Contemporary Spanish Women's Narrative
and the Publishing Industry

Hispanisms

Series Editor

Anne J. Cruz

*A list of books in the series appears
at the back of this book.*

Contemporary Spanish Women's Narrative and the Publishing Industry

Christine Henseler

University of Illinois Press

Urbana and Chicago

Publication of this work was supported by the Program for Cultural Cooperation between Spain's Ministry of Education and Culture and United States' Universities.

♾ This book is printed on acid-free paper.

Library of Congress Cataloging-in-Publication Data
Henseler, Christine, 1969–
Contemporary Spanish women's narrative and the publishing industry /
Christine Henseler.
p.   cm. — (Hispanisms)
Includes bibliographical references and index.
ISBN 0-252-02831-7 (cloth : alk. paper)
1. Spanish fiction—Women authors—Publishing. 2. Spanish fiction—
20th century—History and criticism. 3. Publishers and publishing—Spain.
4. Book industries and trade—Spain. I. Title. II. Series.
PQ6055.H46   2003
863'.6099287—dc21   2002014264

To my mother, Trin-Madlen,
and to my father, Klaus,
for teaching me to reach for the stars
and for giving me the opportunity to do so

Contents

Acknowledgments

If I sit down and write down the names and events of everybody to whom I feel grateful, *Acknowledgments* would become the title of my book. In my twenties, I began to realize just how privileged I was to be able to attend an institution of higher education. This would not have been possible without my mother's courage to give me the push necessary for my feet to hit American soil when I was nineteen years old. My mother inspired me and supported me spiritually and financially every step of the way. She laughed with me in times of success and encouraged me when life pulled me down. I will always be grateful to her. Without my father's sound advice and financial help, my journey would have been more arduous. Thank you both, each in your own special way, for the love and the dedication you have so generously bestowed upon me.

My warmest gratitude goes to the person who has presented me with the greatest gift of all, a life filled with love, happiness, harmony, and adventure: Jan Gorovitz. Jan has been patient with me in times of frustration and caring during times of insecurity and unrest. To her I owe my inspiration and the daily support needed to finish this book. A big thank you also to the support of the many loyal friends, especially to Jane Jilek, Ofelia Ferrán, and Natalia Díaz-Insensé, who have wiped away my tears and listened to my fears, who have called to chat and to show they care, and with whom I have shared so many moments of happiness.

During my academic schooling, I was fortunate to make acquaintance with several professors who believed in me and who encouraged me to learn and improve my skills. I would like to pay special tribute to Robert Spires, Roberta Johnson, and Andrew Debicki. Their mentorship has been essential in the development of my career and I would not be here without them. I am very grateful to Debra Castillo, who continues to guide me with her sound advice and her constant support. I am especially thankful to John Kronik, who, with his green pen, marked every single version of my chapters and articles, two, four, six, and ten times. Without his constructive advice, his grammar lessons, his patience, and his superior expectations, this book would have never come into existence.

I would like to extend a special thank you, for their financial contribution, to the National Endowment for the Humanities and the Program for Cultural Cooperation between Spain's Ministry of Culture and United States' Universities. I would also like to thank the Department of Modern Languages and Literatures and the Dean of Arts and Sciences at Union College for their support and flexibility. Thanks to the SUNY Fredonia Grants Administration Office and the United University Professions for their research support. The following grants, fellowships, and awards from Cornell University allowed me to invest more time to the development of this book here and abroad: the H.C. Berkowitz Fund, the Beatrice Brown Award, the Research Grant, the Student Travel Grant from the Romance Studies Department, the Sage Graduate Fellowship, and the Dissertation Fellowship from the Women's Studies Program. Union College provided financial support for copyright permissions. A special thanks to the Instituto de la Mujer in Madrid for its extremely organized system to provide researchers with information on women's concerns. Thank you also to the publishers Esther Tusquets and Beatriz de Moura, to the Spanish publishing houses that sent me book reviews and interviews, to Berta Bruna for an interview on the marketing of pocket books, and to Laura Freixas and Care Santos, who spent many hours talking and e-mailing me with their insights on the contemporary literary scene. I would like to thank all of the authors in the chapter "Autobiographical Sketches," who devoted their precious time to sitting down and answering my letters and interview questions, and the copyright granting institutions and individuals for allowing me to reproduce their book covers, advertisements, and paintings. I would like to thank the staff at the Interlibrary Loan Departments at Cornell University, SUNY College at Fredonia, and Union College, who so diligently helped me find many articles and books from Spain and elsewhere. I would like to express my gratitude to the University of Illinois Press; to its director, Willis Regier, for adopting this project; to the press's anonymous readers, for their enthusiastic support and immeasurable advice; and for the meticulous job of the copy editor, Katherine Faydash.

I would like to thank all of my family, friends, and colleagues for their constant support and words of wisdom over the years. Those of you who smiled at me and said "hello" as I was walking along the street, on campus, or in the park and those of you who walked next to me for a longer period of time, thank you all for brightening up my world.

Contemporary Spanish Women's Narrative
and the Publishing Industry

Introduction:
Spanish Women Writers and the Book Market

In the past thirty to forty years, the forces of the publishing world have become so influential that it is virtually impossible to analyze novelistic discourses without taking into account the "complex institutional framework
which authorizes, enables, empowers and legitimates [literature]" (Bourdieu
10). Advertisements, best-seller lists, and television and radio interviews with
authors saturate the marketplace and, more often than not, redirect the tastes
and pocketbooks of consumers. Who decides which author is in and which
author is out? If the decision is up to the publishing houses, the canon may be
converted into a financial sheet of accounts. If the decision is up to the readers, the consumers may get lost in the forces of advertising messages.

The globalization of the book market in Spain has contributed to making
the country's publishing industry the third largest in Europe, after Great Britain
and Germany, and the fifth largest in the world. In the year 2000, the market's income exceeded 270 billion pesetas, a 2.7 percent increase since 1999,
and 34 percent of its income was allocated to the publishing giants Planeta,
Planeta–De Agostini, Santillana, SM y Círculo de Lectores.[1] In 2000, in Spain
alone, 30,000 people were employed in publishing—with 3,850 bookstores and
40,000 businesses that sold books, newspapers, paper products, and writing
utensils—and around 60,000 books a year were published, an average of 164
copies a day ("La industria editorial" 37).[2] These volumes were published by
588 houses, of which 24 grossed more than 3 billion pesetas a year, 62.6 percent of the total (Alfieri 12).

Despite this statistical success, many publishers and critics claim that the
publishing industry in Spain is experiencing a crisis, and several of its edi-

tors believe that a reevaluation of the literary market's commercialization is imminent. A globalizing economy, insufficient distribution systems, problems of overstock, political tugs-of-war, new technologies, the Internet, heightened competition, and visual means of entertainment contribute to the changing role of the publishing industry and the direction of the literary enterprise. Most importantly, these coordinates and characteristics shift the position, demands, and expectations of writers who must take the forces of the literary market into account when publishing their works. The problem that the contemporary author faces, according to the Spanish novelist Rosa Montero, is that there is too much noise in the market. The market contaminates the relationship between author and reader and the relationship between author and text. Montero believes that the market is manipulative, loud, and omnipresent. Every writer feels the existence of the fashions and forces of the industry. The obligation of a writer is to resist these pressures and to be on guard "para no caer y no perderte" (so as not to fall and to lose oneself) (e-mail message, 22 July 1998).[3]

While both male and female authors are affected by the emerging demands of the book market, female writers face a particularly complex situation. On one hand, they must resist the discriminatory practices of a traditionally male-dominated literary field, while, on the other hand, they enjoy unprecedented recognition and reception. Laura Freixas, in *Literatura y mujeres,* explains that the media today place special emphasis on literature written by women because the inclusion of female writers in a traditionally male field is still considered a novelty and thus is newsworthy. In a society in which the lack of political and, to some degree, aesthetic ideologies defines literary production, the media place more emphasis on age and gender in categorizing authors (which is why the current generation of writers, born between 1960 and 1975, is called "la narrativa joven" [the young narrative]). Most importantly, says Freixas, in a culture that is highly visual, "las mujeres destacan no sólo por ser minoría sino porque su imagen resulta más llamativa" (women do not only stand out because they are a minority but because their image demands more attention) (*Literatura* 37). Freixas explains that not every woman receives an equal amount or comparative quality of coverage by the media. Differences depend on the medium and on the woman. The more popular a magazine or a television show, the more space the media will provide to a (certain type of) woman. With a more elitist medium, less space will be made available to women. In addition, the more willing a woman is to play certain games, the more attention she will receive from the public. Freixas believes that every woman is free to control her own image, and, in a group of minority professionals (Freixas calculates a 20 percent ratio of female to male writers), the public profile that one novelist chooses resonates in all others (*Literatura* 38). Her argument is supported by the experience of the author Paula Izquierdo who, in the last chapter of this book, "Autobiographical Sketches," discusses the difficulty of being accepted as a serious writer because she is considered physically attractive, and, as such, she must confront questions such as, "If [Lucía] Etxebarría can bare it all, why can't you?"[4]

The publishing panorama that women writers faced in the 1990s displayed characteristics similar to those of the late nineteenth century and the first three decades of the twentieth century.[5] Catherine Davies explains that the social, cultural, and technological changes that took place in the past century "repositioned women in society":

> [They] also inaugurated a boom period in Spanish literature and remapped the relationship between the writer and the reading public. With increasing literacy a potential readership expanded rapidly across class and gender divides. The urban lower-middle and working classes demanded cheap entertainment, provided by a proliferation of magazines, dependent on advertising revenues, and fiction collections set up as commercial ventures. Novels for mass circulation were short and disposable; they were read once only, for pleasure, not for artistic merit. Production increased and many authors—including women—became professionals able to make a decent living from their writings. Their work reached the masses as never before and helped redefine the relations between class, community and nation while actively contributing to the changes in social relationships. (117–18)

Similar to the situation described above, the publishing industry at the end of the twentieth century has experienced a literary boom driven by a capitalist consumer economy. Books are sold like toothpaste in hypermarkets, in megabookstores, and at corner kiosks. Novels are read for their entertainment value by a mass readership looking for "novelas de usar y tirar" (disposable novels). The average edition of a book ranges from one thousand to five thousand copies, and the average shelf life of a book in bookstores ranges from one week to one year. Authors' careers are determined by their exposure to the mass media, and women writers are said to be writing and selling more not because of the literary quality of their books but supposedly because of their star power. In short, the publishing industry is said to be selling out to the financial rewards of best-seller lists and to authors more interested in fame than in writing.

Today's literary establishment echoes the decry of past decades when writers claimed that "the high [had] become *contaminated* by the low, and Spain [was] a *prostitute* who [had] sold out lofty ideas for love of material comforts" (Sieburth 12). The so-called prostitution of the country unabashedly coincides, in both the nineteenth and the twentieth centuries, with the literary opportunities, level of production, and visibility of women writers. Prostitution joins the sale of the (usually) female body with what the *American Heritage Dictionary* (4th ed.) defines as "The act or . . . instance of offering or devoting one's talent to an unworthy use or cause." It is interesting that, in both centuries, the cause—literature—is considered to lose value as women writers enter its folds.

The road to success for female authors has always been a path marked by controversy, invisibility, and (in)difference. One hundred years ago, women writers were making as much news, albeit for different reasons and in different ways, as authors such as Lucía Etxebarría are in the 1990s. Then, as now, women writers had to gain the attention of readers with their erudition, ambition, talent, and often politically controversial display of ideas and narrative styles. They had to break through the male-dominated market by publishing their texts in serialized form, through commercial venues, and in the shape of newspaper and magazine articles. Each writer dealt with a distinct configuration of personal experiences and needs, and professional decisions and opportunities, described extensively in books and articles by Catherine Davies, Roberta Johnson, Janet Díaz, Maurice Hemingway, Mary Lee Bretz, and others. The rise to public recognition, as outlined below, of a few of the most highly regarded female authors of the past century demonstrates that, while the times have changed, many of the factors that lead to the appearance of female authors are still relevant in today's book market.[6]

The success of Emilia Pardo Bazán (1851–1921), baptized "a Lope de Vega in skirts" (Davies 78), is in part due to her aristocratic background, her ambitious and intelligent personality, and her prolific production that began in the popular form of the serial. Pardo Bazán published nineteen novels and more than five hundred short stories; she founded two magazines and a book series and gave innumerable public addresses in forty years. Thick-skinned and resolute, respected for her courage and her powerful writing, Pardo Bazán became the first woman to hold a presidency in the Madrid Athenaeum in 1906, the first woman appointed to the Council of Public Instruction in 1907, and the first female university professor in 1916 (ibid. 78). Pardo Bazán published her first novel, *Pascual López* (1878), in serialized form, and her subsequent books, *Un viaje de novios* (1881) and *La Tribuna* (1883), were disseminated when she was already somewhat a celebrity. Her fame, and her subsequent ability to publish, was founded on her initiative to correspond with and to confront scholars and authors like Marcelino Menéndez Pelayo, Victor Hugo, and José Zorrilla. In 1882 she published a series of articles, *La cuestión palpitante,* in which she supported and explored Émile Zola's theories on naturalism. Her detailed descriptions of childbirth in *Los Pazos de Ulloa* (The House of Ulloa, translated by Davies) (1886) contributed to the outcry of a public who "perceived as obscene depictions of the body (including the female body)" (Davies 81) by no other than a woman. The reaction to her fervent support of naturalism even led to the separation from her husband. With a mother who took care of the household and three children, and with a wealthy aristocratic background, Pardo Bazán was able to continue to write, speak, keep the literary establishment on its toes, and remain in the news. In 1889 her novel *Insolación* "caused so much scandal that she was reputed to be a pornographic writer" (Davies 82). Known for her feminist writings, the publication of two recipe books created so much surprise among her critics that Pardo Bazán remarked: "'Well, what's the matter? Wasn't I an androgynous person, with more andro than gyno? Wasn't it the case that I didn't even know you break an egg before you fry them?'" (qtd. in Davies 85).[7]

Carmen de Burgos (1867–1932) is considered one of Spain's first independent female writers. Because of a series of personal tragedies—an abusive husband whom she left in 1900, the death of her eight-month-old son, and the absence of family connections and financial wealth—de Burgos strove to improve her situation through her career as a teacher and a journalist (Davies 119). Under the pen name "Colombine," de Burgos became "the first woman newspaper reporter [writing for the *Diario Universal*] in Spain and soon reached the public eye with her survey of the divorce question, published in book form as *El divorcio en España* [Divorce in Spain] in 1904" (ibid.). When de Burgos moved to the country's publishing center, Madrid, around 1906, she was asked to collaborate in a weekly series called *El Cuento Semanal.* Her work proved enormously beneficial because "the aim of this commercial venture . . . was to provide short, cheap novels for the increasingly literate public" (Davies 120). From that point, de Burgos built a professional reputation—and, by the 1920s, gained a sizable salary—on the production of thousands of articles, hundreds of books (the majority were novellas and short-story collections), poetry, investigative journalism, and two books of interviews. In her work, she presented "a varied picture of the multiple social tensions from a woman's point of view" (ibid. 136) and personally she defined the "New Woman" (ibid. 126) in an educated as well as a sexually and financially independent manner. Because of her personal circumstances, professional ambition and talent, and "deliberate use of the popular press for didactic purposes" (Pérez 25), de Burgos was able to launch a successful career in the world of literature and feminist politics.

Concha Espina (1869–1955), like de Burgos, owed her literary beginnings to forced and tragic occurrences. In her early twenties, Espina's mother died of pneumonia and her father went bankrupt. Her short and troubled marriage to Ramón de la Serna, their move to Chile, and their insufficient income deprived her of a sense of security that was not restored until she submitted her poetry to a local newspaper called *El Porteño* (Bretz 15). Her publications gave her the confidence to submit other articles to newspapers, such as *El Correo Español* of Buenos Aires, for which she soon became a paid correspondent (ibid.). Upon her return to Spain, Espina continued to write for various Spanish newspapers under a variety of masculine pen names. Following the advice of Marcelino Menéndez Pelayo, she turned to narrative and "won first prize in a local literary competition" with her short story "La riada" (The Rapids, translated by Bretz) (Bretz 17). As Espina's literary career flourished, her relationship with her husband deteriorated to the point of separation. Her move to Madrid as a single, poor mother of five children forced her to make a living off of the sale of her work. *La niña de Luzmela* (The Girl from Luzmela) (1909), published in the form of "the popular *folletín* (serialized novel of the nineteenth century)," allowed for one of her first "[forays] into long fiction" (Pérez 27). *Despertar para morir* (To Wake Up and Die, translated by Bretz) (1910) and *Agua de nieve* (The Woman and the Sea, translated by Bretz) (1911) gained her the attention of publishers, "one of whom attempted to steer her in the direction of the more lucrative erotic novel" (Bretz 18). After the publication of *La esfinge maragata* (Mariflor) (1914), for which Espina won the prestigious Fastenrath Prize, awarded by the Spanish Royal Academy, her success—honors, portraits, and awards—continued without interruption but not without contradiction. Bretz explains that "articles of protest followed the award of the National Prize for Literature" and that "her son Víctor writes with disgust of the literary 'establishment' that remained hostile and resentful of her triumphs" (Bretz 19). Despite such opposition, Espina's talent, ambition, and sense of adventure made her one of the most well known female authors in the first half of the twentieth century.

Rosa Chacel (1898–1994) represents the intellectual woman of the 1920s and 1930s, dedicated not to popular instruction or working-class revolution, feminist or revolutionary politics, but to the aesthetic, ethical, and philosophical elite associated with the avant-garde (Davies 153). Chacel did not write for a mass audience but for an intellectual readership that overwhelmingly comprised men. She was a disciple of Ortega y Gasset, applying his narrative theories to her first novel, *Estación, ida y vuelta* (Station/Season, Round Trip, translated by Pérez), and publishing the first chapter of the same in *Revista de Occidente* in 1928. The novel was not published in its complete form until 1930 (by Ediciones Ulises in Madrid) and was largely ignored by critics. Because of Chacel's lengthy residency abroad (in Italy, Argentina, England, Germany, Greece, France, the United States, Mexico, and Brazil), many of her books were not published in Spain until several years later, and the Spanish literary establishment did not notice her work until she won the Premio de la Crítica in 1976 for *Barrio de maravillas* (Maravillas Neighborhood, translated by Pérez) and in 1977 for *La sinrazón* (Unreason, translated by Pérez). In 1978 she was nominated to the Royal Spanish Academy, and in 1985 she was a contender for the Cervantes prize. It is because of the recognition of these prize-giving institutions that Chacel became one of the most important figures of the twentieth-century Spanish literary scene: "'without her, our literature—that of the Spanish language—would be incomplete'" says Julián Marías (qtd. in Pérez 68).

The development of authors writing in minority languages has a distinct yet similar flavor to the experience of their female colleagues. Mercé Rodoreda (1909–83), hailed by David Rosenthal as "'the most important Mediterranean woman writer since Sappho'" (qtd. in Pérez 82), is often considered one of the most influential Catalan writers of the twentieth century. Rodoreda's withdrawal from school at the age of nine did not stop her from a career in literature and publishing in magazines and newspapers such as *Revista de Catalunya, Clarisme, Mirador, Companya,* and *Meridià* (Pérez 74). Before the Spanish civil war, Rodoreda was in contact with the literary circle of Barcelona, in particular with the Club dels Novellistes, "where she came under the influence of the Sabadell group of vanguardists" (Pérez 74) and began to write novels and short stories. In 1937 her novel *Aloma,* set in prewar Barcelona, was awarded the Crexells Prize and was published by the Institució de les Lletres Catalanes in 1938 (Pérez 77). While this novel hinted at some of the narrative brilliance of Rodoreda's future production, her claim to fame had to wait until many years later. The Republican defeat in 1939 forced Rodoreda into a twenty-three-year exile. Her residency in Bordeaux, Paris, and finally Geneva during the Second World War and the early part of the Franco regime made for a struggling existence without much time to write. She sporadically collaborated in the *Revista de Catalunya,* and, around 1954, in Geneva, she wrote her first important collection, "Vint-i-dos contes" (Twenty-Two Short Stories) that received the Victor Catalá Prize. It is at that time that the quality of Rodoreda's narrative was confirmed, and her success, with *La plaça del Diamant* (1962) (translated as *The Pigeon Girl* in 1967 and *The Time of the Doves* in 1983) was solidified in the public eye.

The success story of Carmen Laforet—the first best-selling author of the post–civil war period—is closely linked to the visibility that accompanies literary prizes. Born in 1921 in Barcelona, Laforet lived in the Canary Islands until 1939, when she moved to Barcelona and then to Madrid (in 1942) to study law and literature. While several of her short stories were published in local journals and some vignettes appeared in the magazine *Mujer* (Woman), Laforet was unknown until the publication of *Nada* (Nothing), which gained her immediate recognition (Johnson, *Carmen*, 24). Among the people whom Laforet asked for advice concerning her manuscript *Nada* was the journalist and critic Manuel Cerezales. He liked the novel and suggested she "submit it to a literary contest that had been created that year in Barcelona" (Gazarian Gautier 155). She followed his advice and won the Nadal Prize. Geraldine Nichols explains that while *Nada* described the deteriorization of the Spanish nation and society, it also applied the same discourse as the Franco regime. Both discourses relied on the myth of the original sin to explain and justify the existence of an asymmetrical world and to structure and give meaning to their respective histories (Nichols, "Caída" 327). For this reason, *Nada* pleased both censors and the public while still upholding some critics' perceptions that the text, written by a young and unknown female writer, remained exactly what its title suggested, "nothing." Despite such opposition, Laforet, at the age of twenty-three, received the Nadal and the Fastenrath Prizes for *Nada* and became one of the most widely read authors in Spain. The experience changed her life and helped her decide to dedicate the remainder of her career to writing texts such as *La isla y los demonios* (The Island and the Devils) (1952), *La mujer nueva* (The New Woman) (1955), *La insolación* (Sunstroke) (1963), *La llamada* (The Call) (1954), and *La niña y otros relatos* (The Child and Other Stories) (1970).

The post–civil war era was particularly difficult for female writers; they had to conform not only to the censoring pens of the Franco regime but also to the restrictive sociocultural environment to which they were to adhere as women. In contrast to Laforet, Ana María Matute (b. 1926) experienced the Spanish civil war firsthand. Partly because of three prolonged illnesses during her childhood and partly because of her family's constant moves between Madrid and Barcelona, Matute expressed her solitude and despair by writing at an early age.[8] In anticipation of her future career and in an attempt to deal with the horrors of the war, Matute, at a very young age, created her own, single-paged magazine, *La Revista de Shybil* (Shybil's Review, translated by Díaz), and wrote two "relatively long compositions, both dated 1938, 'Alegoría' [Allegory] and 'Volflorindo' [no translation]" (Díaz 33). While she wrote several pieces after the war, her first short story, "El chico de al lado" (The Boy Next Door) appeared in the Barcelona magazine *Destino* when she was sixteen years old (Díaz 39). In 1943 "she interrupted her studies of painting and music to devote herself exclusively to literature" (Díaz 39). She wrote *Pequeño teatro* (Little Theater), which remained unpublished for eleven years because "it was taboo in the novels written immediately after the war for any character to commit suicide or adultery" (Díaz 41). Strongly influenced by the novel *Nada,* Matute wrote *Los Abel* (The Abel Family) and submitted it for the Nadal Prize in 1947. It became a finalist for the prize and was published one year later by the Barcelona-based publishing house Destino (which had first contracted to publish *Pequeño teatro* and then retracted the offer). The prize launched Matute's career at the age of twenty-one and gained her favorable interviews in newspapers and on Radio Barcelona (Díaz 44–45). Despite this acknowledgment, Matute had to interrupt her novelistic enterprise and write shorter works to assist her financially during the difficult years of the regime. She wrote during a time that "required unswerving vocation and dedication of a writer, for in Spain this occupation could offer neither artistic nor economic satisfactions: the censor's restrictions and mutilations excluded beforehand any sense of artistic achievement, and the near-total lack of reading public offered little possibility of financial reward" (Díaz 51). It was in the 1950s that Matute received more literary prizes that placed her on the literary map. In 1951 the Tertulia Café del Turia awarded her a grand total of fifteen pesetas for a short story called "No hacer nada" (Doing Nothing), and one year later she won the Premio Café Gijón for *Fiesta al noroeste* (Celebration in the Northwest) (1952), which is considered one of her best novels (Díaz 52). In 1954 Matute's career was established when she received the prestigious Planeta, the Premio de la Crítica, and the Nacional de Literatura. She also received the Nadal Prize in 1959 and the Fastenrath Prize in 1969.

The literary prize, in particular the Nadal, launched the careers of several other post–civil war women writers, including those of Elena Quiroga in 1950, Dolores Medio in 1952, Luisa Forellad in 1953, and Carmen Martín Gaite in 1957 (Carbayo Abengózar 51). The fact that so many women received the Nadal led some to rename it the Premio Dedal (thimble prize) to ironically refer to the sewing instrument to which women were to dedicate themselves instead of writing literature (Carbayo Abengózar 51). The previously mentioned authors had to navigate the personal plights of the civil war and the censoring pens of the Franco regime in order to achieve literary success. Their younger colleagues, including Esther Tusquets (b. 1936), Lourdes Ortiz (b. 1943), Montserrat Roig (1946–91), Carme Riera (b. 1948), Cristina Fernández Cubas (b. 1945), Soledad Puértolas (b. 1947), Rosa Montero (b. 1951), and Rosa Regás (b. 1954), among others, experienced the oppressive strategies of the regime only in part. They were allowed to express their frustrations more freely when the country opened its borders in the 1960s to foreign influences, and the publishing industry, as we know it today, began to take shape. These authors belong to a group called "best-sellers cultos" (cultured best-sellers) (Freixas, *Li-*

teratura 49) because of the power of their name recognition, the literary quality of their work, and their gender. Moving from "cultured" to "contamination," the generation born in the 1960s and 1970s is perhaps most often associated with the "selling out" of the cultural industry. Their life experiences, most detached from the civil war era and the Franco regime, parallel the development of the modern book market (born in the 1960s). For these writers, the mass media and the promotional demands of the industry are a natural part of their lives and therefore novelized in works such as Luisa Castro's *El secreto de la lejía* (The Secret of Bleach) (2001), Lucía Etxebarría's *De todo lo visible e invisible* (Of All That Is Visible and Invisible) (2001), and José Ángel Mañas's *El escritor frustrado* (The Frustrated Writer).

The success of authors in the late nineteenth and early twentieth century was often marked by the adoption of male pen names and by personality traits, such as ambition and erudition, that were portrayed as masculine. Much like female authors today, the literary careers of these authors often began with newspaper, magazine, or journal articles. The publication of serials and short stories functioned then, as now, as a precursor to becoming an author or, according to Carmen Martín Gaite, as an "'apprenticeship for the more serious business of writing novels'" (qtd. in Davies 233). Writers often did not achieve public acknowledgment and success until they were bestowed with a literary prize. What has changed since the late nineteenth century is "not so much the conditions and levels of production, which have improved, but the conditions of reception" (Davies 194). "These days, when women publish their names are registered, their work is taken seriously, accounted for, read, and written about" (Davies 194). A survey conducted by the Ministerio de Educación, Cultura y Deporte (Ministry of Education, Culture, and Sports) concluded that in 2001 more women (58 percent) than men (53 percent) read and that 42 percent of women read more frequently than men (31 percent) ("Barómetro" n.p.). In 1998 the Sociedad General de Autores y Editores (General Society of Authors and Editors) conducted a survey concerning the habits of cultural consumption. The society found that of the 89.5 percent of readers who read fiction, 81.9 percent enjoyed reading contemporary novels (*Informe* 122).[9] The survey concluded that at the end of the twentieth century, the female readership dedicated most of its time to reading fiction (65.8 percent), while the male readership dedicated its time to nonfiction (Sánchez García 126).

Because of these statistics, many editors and critics overrate the privileged position of women writers and the power of female readers. Almudena Grandes, in an article entitled "La conquista de una mirada," states that the increase in female readers is used to support the most varied of hypotheses and is voiced most loudly by male novelists who do not find a welcome audience for their texts. It is not, says Grandes, that male readers have disappeared, but that they are moving into different genres. As such, "los representantes de la élite intelectual, que son básicamente hombres, pero no solamente hombres, afirman sin rubor que no tienen tiempo para leer novelitas" (the representatives of the intellectual elite, mainly, but not solely, men, affirm, unembarrassed, that they do not have time to read novelettes) (Grandes, "Conquista" 61). Despite such fleeting gestures, if one looks at the contents page of a serious literary journal such as *Quimera,* one can easily observe its overarching male constituency. Laura Freixas is one of several author-critics who have pointed to the lack of female writers represented in a given anthology, review, book, or social event. To give just one example of the absence of gender consciousness in literary circles, Freixas describes the following situation: "En Enero de 1993 tuvo lugar en Madrid un 'Encuentro internacional sobre la novela en Europa' que reunió a veinte escritores. El hecho de que todos ellos fuesen varones no suscitó el menor comentario" (In January of 1993, an 'International gathering on the European novel' took place in Madrid that brought together twenty writers. The fact that all of them were men did not provoke one remark) (*Madres* 13).

Some of the most apparent obstacles that women writers must overcome are the sexual politics of elite critics, academics, and journalists who evaluate (works written by) women. Ángeles Caso believes that many prejudices still exist in the twenty-first century, in particular in the predominantly male critical establishment in which "hay cierto tonillo de perdonarnos la vida, de pensar que podías estar haciendo punto de cruz y hacemos novela sentimental" (there is a certain tone of forgiving us life, of thinking that we could be doing needlework and that we are writing sentimental novels) (n.p.). Caso believes that women writers belong to a long tradition in which the work of female authors has been subjected to inappropriate coverage and their minds negate their intellectual capacities.

On a more subtle level, one that suggests the need for an ideological overhaul, Freixas examines the sexist uses of the word *femenino* (feminine) as appropriated by critics in Spanish newspapers and magazines. Her findings conclude that literature written by women is reduced to four distinct categories: (1) feminist, politically incorrect, or opportunist; (2) intimate, emotional, and sensitive; (3) commercial (directed to a wide female readership); and (4) particular, in other words, not universal (Freixas "Lo femenino" 41). In all instances, Freixas demonstrates, through quotes from the Spanish media, that the use of the word *femenino* is largely identified with the marginal and the inferior. Elena Santiago says that there are "editores o críticos de cerrada mentalidad que suponen que si se entusiasman con una autora (femenino) pueden estar provocando alguna sospecha. Es triste, pero ocurre (aún). Sobre esto

11

tengo anécdotas personales que intento olvidar" (narrow-minded editors or critics who assume that if they become enthused with a [female] author they may provoke a certain amount of suspicion. It is sad but it [still] happens. I have personal anecdotes about this topic that I try to forget) (e-mail message, 27 June 1998). Cristina Peri Rossi claims that there are only three reasons why male critics endorse female authors:

1. Que esté interesado en acostarse con ella. No es muy frecuente, porque la pluma [etc.] son símbolos fálicos, de modo que el crítico que se siente atraído por una escritora mujer comienza a sentirse un poco homosexual.
2. Que algún amigo suyo esté interesado en acostarse con esa escritora. Entonces, puede hacer . . . una reseña espléndida, generosa.
3. Si el crítico ya ha quedado impotente, . . . puede hacer una reseña . . . [de] un libro escrito por una jovencita; el fenómeno se llama "paternalismo" y suele desaparecer si la jovencita [saca] algún amante o amanta. (letter, 7 July 1998)

(1. He may be interested in sleeping with her. It is not very frequent, because the pen [etc.] are phallic symbols, whereby the critic who is attracted to a female author begins to have homosexual tendencies.
2. A friend of his may be interested in sleeping with this writer. Then he may write a splendid, generous review.
3. If the critic is already impotent . . . he may write a review of a book by a young author; the phenomenon is called "paternalism" and tends to disappear when the young woman begins to have a boy- or girlfriend.)

We may chuckle (or cry) about these three points of possible male-female professional relationships, but since they are part of Peri Rossi's reality, they suggest that the success or "failure" of literature written by women in Spain is still very much tied to cultural gender associations. One case in point is a story that Peri Rossi tells of a friend whose book presentation was followed by reviews that discussed the beauty of her legs. Her bodily features are highlighted less to sell a product than to undermine the authority of her text.

Lola Beccaria believes that the discriminatory practices of the cultural industry are due to a publishing establishment that was, until several years ago, made up almost exclusively of men: "Eran los hombres los que editaban, los que escogían las obras que se publicaban, los que hacían las críticas, los que llevaban los suplementos culturales de los periódicos, y las revistas culturales y literarias. Por todo ello, se editaban obras que respondieran al gusto de los hombres, a sus preocupaciones e intereses" (It was men who edited, who chose the works to be published, who wrote the critiques, who headed the cultural supplements of newspapers, and the cultural and literary magazines. Because of all of this, men edited the works that correspond to the liking of men, to their preoccupation and to their interests) (e-mail message, 30 July 1999). This situation, as Beccaria mentions, may be changing. Most publishers in the United States, Italy, and Spain (though not so much in Germany and France) count on agents to filter out "bad" or "uninteresting" literature. Authors in these countries are said to find it almost impossible to publish unless they employ the services of a knowledgeable agent—even though reality shows that not all authors employ these services—and in Spain most of these agents are female. Agents have the power to demand appropriate monetary funds, rights, and promotional campaigns for literature that they believe is attractive. Yet, apart from Carmen Balcells, who carried exceptional power in the field, literary agents, says Esther Tusquets, are simply intermediaries.

In a survey that I sent to fourteen publishers in Spain, two female directors of publishing houses were the only ones that responded: Beatriz de Moura from Tusquets Editores and Esther Tusquets from Editorial Lumen. Tusquets enclosed a short article called "La mujer y la edición" (Women and Publishing). In it, she proclaims that because of the large amounts of money involved in the publishing industry, most men are loath to leave it "en manos de estas presuntas irresponsables fantasiosas que somos las mujeres" (in the hands of the supposed irresponsible and conceited women that we are). Despite the environment that Tusquets sketches, it is important to notice the changes that are taking place. While women may not head many publishing houses, they do bring their talents and visions to the industry in other departments. As more women become part of the literary field—in different guises—they take on increasingly powerful positions. It is to be expected, therefore, that literary and cultural studies of works written by women will slowly be given more influential space in journal and newspaper articles and will eventually change the formation of the Spanish literary canon. For example, in 1999 Amaya Elezcano assumed directorship of the prestigious publishing house Alfaguara. She started working for Alfaguara in 1983 as a reader. She continued her career as a style editor and as an assistant director. She is the second woman to become director, after Felisa Ramos. Whether her presence, and the existence of an increasing number of women in the field, will change the destiny of female authors remains to be seen.

What is becoming increasingly more clear is that in the 1990s and the early 2000s, male-dominated institutions and interests have been overshadowed by an industry that is proclaiming a boom in the production and publication of literature written by women. The media functions to cover up the absence of women's full-fledged existence in powerful roles by hyping the power of a select number of women, such as the editors Beatriz de Moura and Esther Tusquets, the literary agent Carmen Balcells, and the writers Espido Freire and Lucía Etxebarría.

Because of biases such as the ones described above, "the reading of literature by women . . . becomes an activity colored by the sharp consciousness that one group is dominant, the other marginal (and often considered inferior), and the forms and functions of literary expression created by the marginal group is most richly read in dialectical opposition to the texts and values of the dominant group" (Ordóñez, "Reading" 241). This dialectical reading has helped to confront the major issues involved in the form and content of female writers' novelistic discourses, and it has allowed authors to unite into a front of resistance and strength. Due to feminist social changes, women have reinserted themselves into the dominant structure and are disrupting the clean opposition that once allowed the concept of a "feminine literature" to enter into existence.

The eclectic approaches of the new generation of writers born in the 1960s and 1970s—Nuria Barrios, Lola Beccaria, Luisa Castro, Lucía Etxebarría, Espido Freire, Belén Gopegui, Begoña Huertas, Paula Izquierdo, Clara Obligado, Carmen Posadas, Carmen Rigalt, Blanca Riestra, Juana Salabert, Care Santos, Marta Sanz, Clara Usón, and others—as well as the more recent work of already known and respected writers from earlier generations suggest that a male-female distinction is inappropriate and outdated. To draw a dividing line between the center and the margin is counterproductive to the contemporary advancement of literature written by women. The dialectical reading suggested by Ordóñez does not take into account that the dominant power—the institutions that make up the market—also gives women's literature a place to establish itself; the industry defines the value of the writer through book reviews, interviews, television spots, prizes, best-seller lists, and academic articles. To leave these forces out of the general picture means forgetting that literature written by women and "[aletada] por el movimiento feminista y por todos los aires renovadoras de los setenta, [alcanzó] un éxito de ventas que, eso sí, llamó la atención de muchos críticos" (propelled by the feminist movement and by the transforming events of the seventies, reached a level of sales that did call the attention of many literary critics) (Nichols, "Mitja" 119). Women writers begin to have the power to contest the dominant structure when they show that they are economically profitable. One way to undermine the dominant (those forces and faces that blindly support works by male writers) is to join the system; by joining it, literature written by women can change the dominant structure and diffuse its initial project. In effect, women writers begin to have the power to contest market coordinates when their work shows itself to be economically profitable.

As female writers move into the limelight of the public eye as well as the publishing eye, they begin to reject the term that once defined their work—"escritura de mujeres." "Women's literature" in Spain is initially evaluated in light of its social-realist dimension because it includes a preoccupation with reform and protest linked to the women's liberation movement and to the post-Franco period. In the 1980s women's literature moved to adopt more personal perspectives and individualistic discursive practices that join textuality with sexuality. As female authors achieve recognition, their unity as an oppositional force disperses, and the authors start to identify more with other male or female writers from the particular genre in which they work (without necessarily withdrawing themselves from "woman-oriented" topics).[10] They also prefer to be identified with a gender-neutral writer. Paloma Díaz-Mas agrees that her work displays feminist concerns, but she rejects the idea of writing or having to write *as a woman*. She believes that after the censorship imposed on authors by the Franco regime, women are in need of communicating their ideas freely without any ties to form, content, or categories: "a las mujeres que escribimos en España en general nos gusta que nos consideren como escritores, o sea, como un escritor que es mujer. Es decir, no hacemos tanto, salvo algunas excepciones, literatura militantemente feminista. A mí me fastidia que me consideren una chica que escribe y que por lo tanto está determinada" (in general, those of us women who write in Spain like to consider ourselves writers: an author who is a woman. In other words, we do not write, apart from a few exceptions, militant feminist literature. I find it annoying that some think of me as a woman who writes and who is thus [biologically] determined) (Ferrán 339).

Many Spanish women writers agree with Díaz-Mas, and they are intent on dismantling the myth of a purely female type of writing. To the question, "¿Considera Ud. su obra una escritura femenina?" (Do you consider your work to be feminine writing?),[11] Ana María Matute, during a 1994 convention organized by the Luis Goytisolo Foundation, answered: "'Yo sólo creo en libros buenos o en libros malos. . . . No obstante, . . . la mujer posee universos de emociones que quizá sólo ella pueda novelar'" (I only believe in good books or in bad books. Nevertheless, . . . woman possesses universes of emotions that perhaps only she can novelize) (qtd. in Rodríguez, "Peri" 37). Ana María Moix proclaimed, in the same year, "'no existe literatura marcada por sexos, [y] la novela femenina entendida como marca de mercado no [me] parece deshonesta siempre que el producto sea bueno'" (literature marked by gender does not exist, [and] I do not consider the feminine novel, understood as a market brand, to be dishonest as long as the product is a good one) (qtd. in Rodríguez, "Soledad" 29). Care Santos, sick of the controversy, says, "Es terrible que siempre se termine hablando del punto de vista femenino y otras estupideces por el estilo" (It is terrible that they always end up talking about the feminine point of view and other stupidities of the same nature) (e-mail message, 15 June 1999). Lucía Etxebarría notes, "'A mí no me avergüenza en lo más mínimo decir que escribo para mujeres, no me parece peyorativo ni discriminador. Pero sí es cierto que nadie le va preguntando a Javier Marías por qué todos sus protagonistas son hombres, ni a Muñoz Molina [por qué] sus libros son tan masculinos. Cada uno utiliza su propia experiencia. No veo por qué yo tengo que ponerme a contar la vida de un señor de 40 años'" (I am not in the least ashamed to say that I write for women; I do not find this pejorative or discriminatory. But it is true that nobody asks Javier Marías why all of his protagonists are men or Muñoz Molina why his books are so masculine. Everyone uses his or her own experience. I do not see why I have to tell the story of a forty-year-old man) (qtd. in Vidal 44). Female authors are proud to present their experiences as women but they agree that the label imposed on them needs to be reevaluated or disregarded in light of the merits of a text.

Many Spanish female authors today resist the notion of being categorized or identified as a "female" writer. The label attached to women writers in the 1980s in particular—"escritura de mujeres" or "literatura femenina"—stigmatizes their work, they say, and pushes them into the status of a social minority.[12] The "special" and double-edged position of "women's literature"—it is at once highly marketed and rendered invisible—makes critics uncomfortable and makes authors wonder whether the category itself may lead women writers into a trap: "Es fácil observar que la mera expresión *literatura femenina* pone incómodo a todo el mundo. Los varones parecen sospechar que las mujeres se escudan en ella para obtener algún privilegio. A menudo se oye murmurar que a calidad igual, es más fácil publicar, o ganar un premio, para una mujer, que para un hombre. Lo cual probablemente es cierto, y vale la pena preguntarse por qué" (It is easy to observe that the mere expression *feminine literature* makes everybody uncomfortable. Men seem to suspect that women hide themselves behind it to obtain some kind of privilege. Frequently, one hears murmurs that, of same quality, it is easier to publish or win a prize for a woman than for a man. This is probably true, and it is worth asking oneself why) (Freixas, *Literatura* 13). Cristina Peri Rossi believes that the reason women's literature is so successful on the market is that "'la literatura ya no ostenta poder. Cuando a los hombres las cosas ya no les importan es cuando llegamos nosotras a ellas'" (literature does not contain power anymore. When men cease to care about things, that is when we women come upon them) (qtd. in Rodríguez, "Peri" 37). Peri Rossi's comment neglects to take into account the basic shift that is occurring in how power is defined. It is not that literature is losing its power but that power is increasingly measured by the number of books an author sells.

As women authors become commercially more visible, their work slowly moves from a negative to a positive pole (first on the market, then—perhaps but not necessarily—on a critical and academic level). Their texts are reviewed on popular television shows as well as in newspapers, magazines, and bookstore windows, with large cardboard images of often seductive-looking individuals. As women authors become commercial icons, their once marginalized status increases their promotional visibility. Viewed from a market standpoint, the initial project of women's literature—dependence on a new concept of reading and reading for difference not as deficient but as self-defining (Ordóñez, "Inscribing" 45)—becomes real as difference is mainstreamed and used to increase profits: "Difference sells."[13] In the past two years, Lucía Etxebarría has become a central public figure, associated with a purely profit-oriented business that makes many authors and critics question the validity of her work. Ironically, because of the marketing network that surrounds her, her novels are gaining value as manifestations of a new realist and female-oriented expression. In academic circles, classes entitled "Contemporary Spanish Women Writers" or "Contemporary Spanish Narrative" are incorporating Etxebarría's *Amor, curiosidad, prozac, y dudas* (1997), *Beatriz y los cuerpos celestes* (1998), or *Nosotras que no somos como las demás* (1999) as a continuation and redefinition of the tradition of "feminine literature." That body of literature must then be renamed to the effect of "feminine production" to include both the product and the almost theatrical production that surrounds the success of (female) contemporary authorship.

Literature written by women takes part in a structure determined by the continually changing coordinates of the market. According to an individual writer's character, background, and financial and personal situations, the author reacts in relation to the set of forces—political, economic, social, popular—that determine the cultural production of the literary field at a particular time in history. These forces shift in relation to one another. Pierre Bourdieu believes that internal changes are not possible without external ones: "Changes which affect the structure of the field as a whole, such as major reorderings of the hierarchy of genres, presuppose a concordance between internal changes, directly determined by modification of the chances of access to the literary field, and external changes which supply the new producers . . . and their new products with socially homologous consumers" (55). In other words, should an extraordinary murder shake the population, the detective novel may take on new characteristics. Should an author inherit a large amount of money, he or she may be able to approach a particular subject matter, style, or genre with a more independent attitude toward the industry and thus bring about the creation of a new collection of texts. In the same vein, works in one particular subgenre may change in relation to other works produced in that same subgenre.[14] For instance, the success in 1989 of *Las edades de Lulú* by Almudena Grandes allowed the lesser-known Mercedes Abad to find a place more easily in the world of female erotic literature.[15] Clara Obligado, on the other hand, had a very difficult time finding a publisher for her erotic-historical-feminist text *La hija de Marx* in part because of the nonexistence of this particular literary genre.

While institutional practices certainly frame authors' lives to a certain degree, one must not erase the power of an individual's agency in the establishment of her and her colleagues' literary fate. In this work, I propose to open the discussion of the effects that the forces of the literary market have on the production of literature written by women. The analysis presented in each of the six chapters of this study is interdisciplinary in its approach. The novels by Paloma Díaz-Mas, Lourdes Ortiz, Cristina Peri Rossi, Esther Tusquets, Almudena Grandes, and Lucía Etxebarría are interpreted on two different levels—the visual and the verbal—and in relation to the promotion of both of those levels. The visual level accounts for the creation of a seductive female body both within and outside of the text. The verbal level refers to discourse's promotional application of that female body on a narrative level. This study joins marketing and visual culture to highlight the seductive power of the female image in present-day marketing philosophies. The advertisement or book cover that introduces each chapter serves as a metafictional, or metavisual, device to remind readers of the limitations and powers at work in the construction of the female body and the body of writing by women novelists. Chapters 1 through 4 tease out the visually constructed female body from under its text-based referents. Chapters 5 and 6 allow the promotion of the extratextual female body, that of the authors, to take part in the redefinition and repositioning of literature written by women. In the final chapter, women writers step out from behind the pages of their books to talk about the influence of the publishing industry on the changing content of their works and on their self-definitions as writers. "Autobiographical Sketches" gives space to the voices of Lola Beccaria, Paloma Díaz-Mas, Espido Freire, Paula Izquierdo, Rosa Montero, Clara Obligado, Care Santos, and Marta Sanz. The objective of *Contemporary Spanish Women's Narrative and the Publishing Industry* is to place women's literature in a new paradigm and to understand the way women writers react—on a textual and on a promotional level—to the changing demands of the book market and the making of the literary canon.

Notes

1. In 1997 Planeta controlled seventy businesses, including Ariel, Seix-Barral, Destino, Deusto, Espasa Calpe, Martínez Roca, Temas de Hoy, and Tusquets (Langa Pizarro 37).

2. Of the 3,850 bookstores in Spain, 766 are located in Catalonia, 510 are in Madrid, 508 in Andalusia, 349 in Galicia, 334 in the province of Valencia, and 237 in Basque Country ("La industria editorial" 37).

3. The translation is my own, as are all subsequent translations not otherwise attributed.

4. The chapter 6 herein provides a detailed study of the promotion of Etxebarría and her reasons for "baring it all."

5. Roberta Johnson, in "Narrative in Culture, 1868–1936," says: "According to Jean-François Botrel, there were more than 2,000 novelists in Spain in the nineteenth century. Many authors enhanced sales by writing serial novels, and the installment format had a hand in shaping the length of works and their plots" (124). For more information on the development of the book market and for statistics on women as readers in the 1830s and 1840s, see Kirkpatrick.

6. I begin this short overview with Pardo Bazán because she is the first, most influential, woman writer of the Castilian language who wrote during the publishing "boom" of the nineteenth century. Other authors such as Cecilia Böhl von Faber (also known as Fernán Caballero, 1796–1877) and Rosalía de Castro (1837–85), no doubt left an important mark on the development of literature written by women before Pardo Bazán. Other influential female writers that I do not portray here are Caterina Albert, Carmen Conde, Gertrudis Gómez de Avellaneda, María Teresa León, Concha Méndez, Federica Montseny, and María Zambrano, among others. This overview serves to highlight some of the most important Spanish women writers before the contemporary period and why the succeeded; it does not claim to give a detailed account of their personal lives or professional careers.

7. The information presented on Pardo Bazán derives from Davies.

8. The information presented on Matute derives from Díaz.

9. Within this category, 37.3 percent read adventure novels, 35.1 percent historical novels, 21.4 percent science fiction novels, 20.2 percent detective novels, 17.3 percent sentimental novels, 12.3 percent best-sellers, 12.3 percent folkloric texts, and 10.2 percent novels noire (*Informe* 122).

10. Rosa Montero affirms this move in the following statement: "las obras (las mías y las de todas) se van clasificando más, en efecto, en el género de la obra en sí" (the works [mine and those of everybody] are being, in effect, increasingly classified according to the genre of the work itself) (e-mail message, 23 July 1998).

11. Carmen Martín Gaite has spoken extensively about the scope of a particularly feminine literature. See *Desde la ventana* for four of her talks about this issue given at the Fundación Juan March.

12. This extensively discussed term—*feminine literature*—links women's biological essence to certain narrative techniques and topics (e.g., *écriture féminine*, circularity, fantasy, the oral tradition, the short story, the diary, the autobiography, and so on). It subverts traditional male value systems, redefines female sexuality, reevaluates matrilinear roots, recognizes the interests of female readers, and questions women's contested passive and objective status as readers, writers, viewers, and speakers. The

impact of these issues has crossed oceanic divides; it has moved among academic, social, political, and cultural spheres; it has been corporealized in live bodies and in textual experiments; it has been analyzed from all angles; and it has penetrated some of our discussions to the point of saturation.

French feminist theory has not had as strong an impact in Spain as in other countries such as the United States and Great Britain. It can be seen, as Ordóñez explains in "Inscribing Difference: 'L'Écriture féminine' and New Narrative by Women," to echo in the 1980s in discussions about the essence and difference of feminine literature in Spain. See Threlfall for more information about the impact of the women's movement in Spain.

13. Women writers and their relationships with the forces of the publishing industry, that is their position vis-à-vis literary critics, agents, editors, marketing directors, and journalists, is a field that has just recently been tapped into by authors such as Laura Freixas in *Literatura y mujeres,* and novelists like Lucía Etxebarría in the prologue of *Nosotras que no somos como las demás* and *La letra futura.* While scholarly writings are not prolific on the subject, Spanish newspaper articles, book reviews, and interviews with women writers disclose a growing concern surrounding the representation of female writers in the media.

14. Care Santos says, "Está claro que el género [la escritura femenina] puede condicionarnos como seres humanos, también como creadores" (It is clear that the genre [feminine writing] can condition us as human beings, and as creators) (e-mail message, 15 June 1999).

15. The success of *Las edades de Lulú* made publishers aware of the economic benefits of the erotic genre and opened the door for other female erotic writers.

1

Vision over Truth:
El sueño de Venecia by Paloma Díaz-Mas

A visual image is an inherent part of the promotional appeal of a book and an author. The cover of *El sueño de Venecia* by Paloma Díaz-Mas reproduces a section of the painting *Mariana of Austria* by Diego Rodríguez Velázquez (fig. 1). The reproduction uses a similar technique as an advertisement that displays *La Gioconda* by Leonardo da Vinci to sell Conde de Osborne brandy (fig. 2): both crop a classical painting and position it within a newly contextualized frame. The book cover serves to link the readers' perception of the book to the painting described in the text, and it functions at a glance to position Díaz-Mas's novel as a historical novel or, as the back cover indicates, a "Historia revelada en historias" (a history revealed in histories). On the book and in the ad, a classical painting is recontextualized and reduced to a cutout section that intends to emphasize and give value to the product being sold.[1] The female body is used in each recontextualized instance as a source of redefined meanings and parodic supplements. The well-known paintings serve to attribute authority to each product and seduce a certain audience into wanting to consume the product and know its enigma. Seen purely as products, both books and brandy move through some of the same channels of production, dissemination, and consumption—"'se vende mi libro como se puede vender pasta de dientes'" (my book is sold similar to the way toothpaste is sold), says the psychiatrist Carlos Castillo del Pino (qtd. in Castilla and Rubio 31). Indeed, more than one person may find enjoyment savoring a glass of brandy while reading a good novel—after picking both up at the local grocery store.

The brandy ad discloses a move from what its viewers know to be unmanipulated representations of images located in their original context—such

PALOMA DÍAZ-MAS

El sueño de Venecia

Premio Herralde de Novela

ANAGRAMA
Narrativas hispánicas

Figure 1.   Book cover of *El sueño de Venecia* by Paloma Díaz-Mas (1992) with detail from Diego Rodríguez Velázquez's *Mariana of Austria*. (Reprinted with the permission of Anagrama)

Figure 2. Advertisement for Conde de Osborne brandy, "El enigma de los enigmas," created by Lorente Grupo de Comunicación in 1997. (Original of the campaign Brandy Conde de Osborne with authorization from Osborne and Cia)

as museums, galleries, churches, or castles—to that of recontextualized representations in ads and on posters, cereal boxes, or television that are fragmented and reappropriated for contemporary commercial means (see Benjamin). Consumers are used to reproductions of originals that, as John Berger indicates, they always see out of context (19). A painting is transformed when a detail is isolated, when text is added in a posterlike fashion, and when an artwork is taken out of its so-called natural surrounding and placed in living rooms or on city walls. A simple look at book covers shows that examples of this transformation abound in the publishing industry: *La sombra del triángulo* (Anagrama, 1996) by J. A. Masoliver Ródenas reproduces a 1945 painting by Max Beckmann called *La carta*; *Bella y oscura* (Seix Barral, 1993) by Rosa Montero displays George Grosz's *La calle*; *Todos mienten* (Anagrama, 1993) by Soledad Puértolas reproduces Robert Reid's 1899 *Fleur-de-Lis*; and *Siete miradas en un mismo paisaje* by Esther Tusquets (Lumen, 1981) reproduces Andrew Wyeth's 1948 *Christina's World*. In addition, many more novels, such as Juan Manuel de Prada's *La tempestad* (Planeta, 1997) and Manuel Vázquez Montalbán's *El estrangulador* (Mondadori, 1994), reproduce paintings on the first few pages and on the covers of the books that function as central, unifying visuals for the argument of the novel—somewhat like an internalized promotion. In all of these cases, the "image reproduced has become part of an argument which has little or nothing to do with the painting's original independent meaning" (Berger 28). An image that is taken out of context and transformed, overlapped, or fragmented forces readers and viewers to question its origins.

In the case of *El sueño de Venecia* (The Dream of Venice), viewers of the book cover reside in constant, confusing flux between their internal interpretations and external marketing influences. The viewers are the source of a playful interchange of bordering realities in which the large, bold-faced title of the novel complements the black skirt in the reproduced detail of the painting. The cover joins the textual and the visual; it connects the present of the readers' positions with the past of their learned experiences and hurtles them into new dimensions, as the topic of the dream—Venice—takes them into exotic, modernist scenes or personal psychoanalytic explorations. The title calls attention to the possibility of a shift from the pure exposition of dreamlike *content* to the importance of the *act* of dreaming. The title signals an unconscious transgression of known and unknown paradigms through the act of interpretation, and the cover tries to disrupt the readers' sense of direction in a city in which canals, or aquatic streets, are substituted for cement, earthly streets. The cover brings to life what was mere text and image; it creates a multidimensional form that is "caught in a perpetual metamorphosis; since there is no meaning without displacement of meaning, without metaphor, there is no form without changes of form, without metamorphosis" (Focillon 26). The cover is one in which the restlessness of fragmented and juxtaposed discourses is complemented by the readers' own visual and textual interpretations.

Within the novel, the visual dimension of "el sueño de Venecia" is played out through a painting that occupies the entire last chapter and is its central topic. In the four earlier chapters, the painting is a marginalized element that pulls all five stories together into a body of text, a novel. The painting described in the narrative can be confused with the fragment of Velázquez's painting *Mariana of Austria* reproduced on the book cover (fig. 3), because the ever changing meaning of the painting in *El sueño* represents "the ideology of the inexhaustible work of art, . . . the fact that the work is indeed made not twice, but a hundred times, by all those who are interested in it, who find a material or symbolic profit in reading it, classifying it, deciphering it, commenting on it, combating it, knowing it, possessing it" (Bourdieu 111). Through the visual image, Díaz-Mas's novel undermines the authority of the original painting and emphasizes the metamorphosing position of the artwork within the field that authorizes it. The painting also ascertains the position that its painter and, by extension, Díaz-Mas may occupy as they are determined by the institutional frameworks that value their work.

El sueño uses the promotional power of the female image in the painting to unify and connect the five stories that make up the novel. In each chapter, the female body in the painting is recontextualized and parodies the gendered use of art for propagandistic purposes. The parody works on two levels: it goes back in time to critique the authority of language, and it goes forward in time to comment on the power of the visual image.[2] In all five chapters, the narrative bears a relationship to the visual as the text and the female image become the site of absolute truths, propagandistic subversions, phenomenological premonitions, psychological perversions, and inquisitorial reinscriptions. The characters project their needs, horrors, and desires onto a canvas that is distorted, cropped, and obscured through time and is converted in each instance into a distinct moment of originary signification. The text becomes the site at which vision creates meanings, versions, and distortions as the visual image is reduced to language. The superimposition and undermining of the text by the visual destabilizes the concept of truth and positions the readers within a realm dominated by the image. The painting exemplifies the manner in which the visual determines the production of meaning, the way Velázquez's painting on the cover is used to sell *El sueño.*

Díaz-Mas uses parody, pastiche, collage, and juxtapositions to point to the female body as a source that can produce new meanings. The author's return to the past in *El sueño* "no es nostálgico, sino que, al contrario, cuestiona sus

Figure 3.   Diego Rodríguez Velázquez, *Mariana of Austria.* (Musée du
Louvre, Paris; 87EE1617; copyright Réunion des Musées Nationaux/Art
Resource, New York)

contradicciones y paradojas y, al hacerlo, pone también en tela de juicio, el presente" (is not nostalgic, but the opposite; it questions its contradictions and paradoxes and, by doing so, it unsettles the present) (Hernández 454). Díaz-Mas juxtaposes time frames and systems of signification (the textual and the visual); she takes them beyond parody to the limits of the text and beyond the reach of interpretation by emphasizing the self-reflexive irony of language.[3] The female body that is textually distorted in each chapter is "now regarded as the sort of sign that presents a deceptive appearance of naturalness and transparence concealing an opaque, distorting, arbitrary mechanism of representation" (Mitchell, *Reconfigured* 8). The irony of the novel's message lies in its parody of the visual and textual representations of the female body.

Readers of *El sueño* walk hand in hand with the visual and the textual through a novel that challenges their unequivocal desire to observe and know the abstract in absolute terms. Díaz-Mas's readers can question my thesis developed on the following pages and find what falls between the cracks of my reading. My approach imitates the experiences of viewer and character, not that of the reader. I begin with the novel's epigraph and the fifth chapter and work backward—through the fourth chapter to the first—thus creating a frame for the painting that readers of this study are about to see. My investigation confronts first the outermost layer, the surface of the page or canvas, and intends to uncover the layers of paint, content, parodies, and histories buried beneath it, instead of beginning with the first word and following it to its narrative conclusion. This procedure is an effort to emulate the character in the fifth chapter of the novel, who would have to read *El sueño* from finish to start in order to uncover the layers of the painting he is interpreting. My approach is also the process in which the readers of *any* narrative are invited to engage after finishing the text's last word.

⁓

The epigraph to the novel, supposedly taken from a 1651 text by Esteban Villegas, serves as a framework for *El sueño*. The fable presented in the epigraph, an invention of Díaz-Mas's, sets up from the beginning the impossibility of a truthful interpretation:

Vi entonces aparecer ante mis ojos una Doncella de peregrina hermosura, aunque ciega. Guiábala un Viejo venerable, el cual en su mano izquierda portaba un cedazo. Apenas hubieron llegado a la ribera del río de la Historia, cuando la Doncella se inclinó muy graciosamente y a tientas comenzó a tomar grandes puñados de las arenas de oro que allí había, y a echarlas en el cedazo con mucha diligencia; y el viejo cernía aquella arena como quien ahecha. Mas como el oro era menudo y la criba gruesa, íbasele el oro por el cedazo al río y tornaba a perderse en las aguas, mientras que él se quedaba sólo con los gruesos guijarros que entre la arena había, los cuales guardaba en su zurrón como cosa de mucha estima. Demandé al Desengaño, mi guía, cuál era el enigma de aquella vista, y él me respondió con muy gentil y grave continente:

—Has de saber que esta Doncella, tan hermosa como desdichada, es la Verdad; a la cual los dioses, allende la crueldad de hacerla ciega, diéronla otra grave pena, y es la de no ser nunca creída; testigo de lo cual es aquella profetisa Casandra, que cuanto mayor verdad profetizaba menos creída por los de Troya. Mas porque no se despeñase ni desapareciese del todo del mundo, otorgaron los dioses a la Verdad ese viejo como destrón, el cual es el Error, que nunca se separa un punto de ella y siempre la guía. El cedazo que lleva es la humana Memoria, que, como criba que es, retiene lo grueso y deja escapar lo sutil. (11–12)

[I then saw appear before my eyes a blind maiden of peculiar beauty. A venerable old man, who in his left hand held a sieve, guided her. Just having arrived at the shore of the river of History, the maiden graciously bent down, blindly started taking handfuls of golden sand kernels found there, and diligently threw them into the sieve; and the old man sifted the sand like a winnower. But since the gold was small and the screen wide, the gold fell from the sieve back into the river and was lost again in the waters; he was left only with the large pebbles that remained in the sand, which he saved in his pouch as an element of much esteem. I asked Enlightenment, my guide, what the enigma of this vision was, and he answered in a gentile and grave countenance:

"You should know that this maiden, as beautiful as she is unfortunate, is the Truth, to whom the gods, besides the cruelty of blinding her, gave another grave punishment, namely that of never being believed. Testimony of this is the prophet Cassandra who was less believed by the Trojans the more truth she predicted. So that Truth would not totally give up or disappear, the gods gave her this old man, who is Error, as an annoyance; he never separates himself from her and he always guides her. The sieve that he holds is the human memory that, as the screen that it is, retains the coarse and lets the subtle disappear."]

It is essential to note that the sieve represents human memory and that the larger pebbles trapped in it are carefully guarded in the old man's jacket. What memory leaves behind therefore is kept by Error. Memory in Error's pocket abandons history and is constructed by each individual in relation to the unknown other. The other will always be extraneous and different, as well as never totally visible, never attainable, never fully understood; but without the hand that guides them, the readers are only "*Is*," or "eyes," who cannot see or walk beyond a few steps.

The novel begins with those particles of sand that the old man keeps in his pouch "as an element of much esteem"—but, what is of "much esteem" when retained by the hand of Error? When Truth is metaphorically placed in the hands of a blind maiden led by Error, light and darkness are forever intertwined in obscured meanings. This chiaroscuro relationship limits the readers' vision; it shows that their all-knowing sight can create obscurity, that is, the error of reading the epigraph as a true historical document. The readers find themselves jumping in and out of light, falling into shadows, blinded by light one second and darkness another. Those meanings obscured by blind spots fall through the cracks of phonology, syntax, and semantics as they reduce vision to language.

The epigraph sets up the relationship between truth and vision by pointing to the blind spots within which contemporary readers and viewers are positioned. The development of sophisticated photographic and cinematic techniques, such as digital technology, have changed the so-called real into an apparition of the constructive quality of vision. Postmodern vision is filled with uncertainty, fantastic overlappings, and fragmentation because the product intertwines fact and fiction, still images and movement, third-person and first-person narratives, and it erases characters' and viewers' boundaries. This process has made viewers interrogate their definitions of what is real and what is not, what is historical and what is fictitious. The eye is a lens that reproduces only a carefully chosen amount of information; it is artificially finite and reproducible. Vision can critique itself, as well as the viewers' position, how they see, and the objects or subjects they perceive. The way in which modern technology has reconstructed the human eye and re-presents what is real and true makes vision collapse upon itself; it is inverted and loses its all-seeing attributes. By connecting truth to error and vision, Díaz-Mas's epigraph points to a chiaroscuro, scotomatous relationship based on subjective points of view and infinite recontextualizations.

In the epigraph, the readers are reminded that any time they believe to have located truth, their next step will refute that truth or reveal that the truth is based on erroneous presuppositions—a conclusion they might reach as they discover the title of the painting and the painter on the third page. The readers are left in a position from which they reconstruct the fragment of the painting based on the system they use to describe themselves and others. Language becomes their medium of identification; they try to create truth by naming it. They describe it, they meticulously study it, they justify it, and, through the act of naming it, they reflect on their inability to recreate it.

The narrator of the fifth chapter believes to have uncovered the truthful origin of a painting from the sixteenth century. His use of the impersonal "se," together with phrases such as "sin duda" (without a doubt) (207), "acertadamente supone" (correctly presupposes) (212), and "no hizo más que confirmar la primera impresión" (did nothing more than confirm the first impression)

(208), reinforce a narration that is to appear objective and, above all, true. The narrator explains that the artwork came from the Benedictine convent of San Plácido, but before that had been found beneath a coffee table in a Sevillan home, hidden from the terrors of the civil war. The painting, he believes, represents two daughters of the Jewish couple Alfarache-Osorio: the seated Doña Rufina de Alfarache, eighteen years of age, and, standing at her side, her younger sister, Ana, sixteen years of age. The canvas was cut, leaving only the hand of the younger sister on the shoulder of Doña Rufina. An amateur painter some time ago had turned the image of Doña Rufina into that of the Virgin Mary "por el sencillo procedimiento de añadir una aureola dorada en torno a su cabeza" (by the simple procedure of adding a golden halo around her head) (208–9). The amateur painter also placed on her lap an image of the child Jesus and a dove on top of the hand. The narrator attributes a Z, the only indication of the identity of the painter, to Velázquez's friend and fellow student Baltasar Zabala, who lived in Seville between 1598 and 1670. The narrator insists that this supposition has been verified *without a doubt* by research into the style, technique, coloring, and historical reference of the painting.

Yet the reason for the removal from the painting of the youngest sister cannot be explained. The narrator attributes the deletion to a family disgrace: the younger sister became the lover of the count of Villamayor and later mistress to King Felipe IV. Doña Rufina, struck by grief over her sister's fate, entered a convent (it is not clear if there was a direct connection between these two events). Her father, Baltasar, "quiso conservar el retrato de su hija monja cuando aún estaba en el mundo, pero eliminando el doloroso recuerdo de la muchacha seducida" (wanted to conserve the portrait of his nun daughter when she was still alive but eliminate the painful memory of the seduced girl) (220), so he excised her image, leaving the canvas in its present state. The narrator identifies the painting's historical context, content, and originator; he says that he is able to reconstruct "cabal y verazmente la historia anterior de la muchacha y de su familia" (precisely and truly the former history of the girl and her family) (221). He brings to the surface a memory that has been eliminated, thrown away, cut out, and painted over. The narrator rewrites and testifies to history, which, as Bill Readings put it, "amounts to the deconstruction of the binary opposition between voice and silence, history and the unhistorical, remembering and forgetting. It's a history directed toward the immemorial, to that which cannot be either remembered (represented) or forgotten (obliterated)" (62). The readers enter into a mnemonic process that begins with a scientific and academic account of a newly discovered interpretation and plunges into a deconstruction of that interpretation's founding binaries.

The readers can chuckle at the academic's misinterpretations because they have the privilege of knowing who is really depicted in the painting. But when placed into the scholar's position or that of a contemporary viewer, readers find themselves confronted with a situation similar to the one exposed in the novel. Just as the painting by the unknown "Z" is relocated within the known and overdetermined history of Velázquez, the cover image by Velázquez provokes a spurious association with the textual description of the painting. The readers, and the academic in the fifth chapter, believe they have identified the relation between the book cover and the painting by Zabala as well as the image that reaches the consumers and the academic in the form of a book or a cut-up piece of canvas. In each case, the cultural context is transformed, historical references are erased, and signs are resignified to fit into contemporary systems of appropriation. As the archaeological endeavor of the academic demonstrates, his "scientific" methods are part of an overall reevaluation of the extent to which, according to Díaz-Mas, "'nuestra visión del pasado puede ser objetiva, o está mediatizada por nuestra visión del presente'" (our vision of the past can be objective or it is mediated by our vision of the present) (qtd. in Ferrán 328).

In the fourth chapter, the propagandistic dimension of the female body is made visible. The painting takes on a secondary role and is not described until the end of the chapter. It is seen only through the eyes of a little girl who has converted the back of a wooden coffee table into a site of imaginary adventures for herself and her hero, Capitán Trueno, a cartoon character. Beneath the coffee table, the little girl confronts "los Ojos Malos" (the Evil Eyes)— eye-shaped wood markings—her imaginary enemy and a parodied version of the "evil eyes" of the Franco regime. The table is covered over, transformed, and distorted by a painting that is hidden beneath it.[4] The painting depicts the Virgin Mary with a halo around her head, the child Jesus on her lap, and a dove on her shoulder. The fantastic space of the table and, by extension, the mind of the little girl are subtly replaced by religious images that substitute a masculine game of heroes and combat for a feminine system of behavior based on passivity, purity, and obedience. Art, in this case, is deformed in order to influence the mind of the young girl, and it is naturalized once she internalizes the symbols. The girl's imagination is censored and replaced by doctrines of the Franco regime. The imaginary fight against the "Ojos Malos" turns into a real fight against (or automatic acceptance of) those eyes of the *Sección Femenina* that constantly and closely watch the physical and mental behavior of Spanish women.[5]

In this chapter, the erotic appeal of the female nude is transformed into appropriate forms of social representations without forfeiting the promotional appeal of the female body. The painting is converted into a propagandistic poster. Its transformation is visually ironic, much like Goya's provocative nudes or the openly sexual gaze and playfully masturbating hand of Titian's *Venus of Urbino*. The hands of Francoist censors metaphorically are made visible as they try to eradicate those hands that seem too mysterious, ambiguous, and provocative. The text of the chapter locates the characters in a time—the fifties and sixties—when foreign industries began to influence the mass media monopoly of Francoist Spain. The consumer mentality is expressed through Cola-Cao radio jingles, lyrical ad songs by José Luis, and cartoon figures. The text proposes a contradictory representation of the ideal figure of Spanish womanhood in relation to more liberated images inspired by the North American advertising industry.

While in the fifth chapter the painting is reduced to a scientific discourse, in the fourth chapter the text adopts propagandistic traits that dissolve the power of the fifth chapter's narrative and together with the power of the visual image express a new system of censored and subversively manipulative significations. This fusion reflects the artificial boundary between that which proclaims the "trueness" of the academics discoveries and that which points to the image's equally "true" or self-evident meaning of prescribed propaganda for female behavior. In this process, readers glimpse the postmodern tendency to rewrite history as anachronism, "a kind of temporal anamorphosis, in which the present event of writing is not eliminated by the past event that is written about, or vice versa. Rather, two heterogeneous temporalities are co-present" (Readings 58). Creating and encoding signifiers does not follow a neat chronological pattern that slowly uncovers or discloses more truths; rather, interpretation disrupts and interrupts in an uncanny fashion new patterns of signification that are continuously recontextualized and reappropriated. Lyotard relates this idea to Freud's *Nachträglichkeit,* which refers to a deferred or displaced event that "'occurs too soon to be understood, and is understood too late to be recovered'" (qtd. in Readings 59). The little girl who is confronted with the painting underneath the table cannot yet understand the significance of the blue eyes that soon are to take hold of her imaginary capabilities, nor can the academic in the fifth chapter comprehend their significance, because he stands before a painting after it has been recast with an entirely new set of disclosed meanings. Nevertheless, both characters are confronted with temporal truths that intermingle the visual and the textual. From the fifth to the fourth chapter, the visual and the textual begin to intertwine, to interiorize each other's discursive powers and "bring to light and articulate the various (indirect) ways in which the two domains do indeed implicate each other, each one finding itself enlightened, informed, but also affected, displaced, by the other" (Felman 8).

In the third chapter, the canvas brings to the forefront that which is verbally inexpressible and the power that lies in the phenomenological experience of the visual, as in feelings, desires, and premonitions. This complicated chapter revolves around an act of incest, unknown to the couple involved, Álvaro and his daughter Isabel. The painting that is situated above their wedding bed is the one the readers are familiar with, but it is now in a more "originary" state, for it does not include the clumsy addition of the Virgin Mary, the child Jesus, or the dove. The painting has acquired a greenish tint because it was varnished for better conservation. Because it was too large, the owner cropped it so that he could carry it with him more easily on a trip to Havana. The cutout figure was, as Alvaro says, that of a young boy about his own age—fifteen—when he left for Cuba. In eliminating this image, he leaves on the shoulder of the other figure a hand that Isabel interprets as "un signo de mal agüero" (a bad omen) (142). Alvaro makes fun of this feeling by asking Isabel for her own white hand. The painting then functions as an unconscious mirror in which a premonition is turned into a real-life situation. As scientific and propagandistic layers are peeled away from every subsequent version of the image, the painting brings to the surface hidden signs that move the viewers closer to a genesis, an interior revelation of being that goes beyond textual authority and is slowly possessed, haunted by the unknown, the enigma. When Alvaro commits suicide and leaves a letter behind that explains the truth of the incestuous situation, Isabel hides it immediately. His text is suppressed while she keeps until her own death the painting that she once so abhorred. The truth then resides in the painting, not in the letter, where conventional meanings reside, but where opacity and the unrecognizable dominate. After every chapter of the novel, the visual further opens the space of signification for viewers of the painting by reducing its textual meaning to an aberration that becomes more abstract and intuitive, more phenomenological and psychologically influenced, more open to the visual.

The importance of this chapter lies in the enigmatic presence of the hand as a form that determines the disposition of the protagonists. The hand parodies the text as a whole; it uses the body as an erotic and enigmatic site of multiple meanings. When hands, lips, breasts, legs, thighs, and other body parts are employed in ads, they represent particular gender displays, understood by Erving Gofman as conventionalized portrayals of culturally established correlates of sex (iv). The body part, says Gofmann, is a display that "is lifted out of its original context, parenthesized, and used in a quotative way, a postural resource for mimicry, mockery, irony, teasing" (vi). Viewers and readers readily reduce the female body and the body of literature to this one part.

In the second chapter, the power of language is undermined even more. The authority of the protagonist's discourse is questioned as readers compare his letters to his desire for a woman in a painting. As the feelings and actions of the protagonist, Lord Aston-Howard, are transferred from the painting to a human being, his intentions to possess the female figure in the painting fail, and the hypocrisy of his person is exposed. The English Lord Aston-Howard traveled to Spain and described in a series of letters to his friends, his wife, and his lover the deterioration of the country.[6] The events of the chapter take place in the nineteenth century during a period of disintegration in the Spanish royal house of the Bourbons, just before the uprising of 1808. Readers become aware of the relationship between historic deterioration and the decadent Lord Aston-Howard himself: the only thing that the lord has is his title, the only thing that he is interested in is economic value, and the only thing that he can communicate to the readers through his letters is his extreme hypocrisy. For example, he comments on the typical large-winged hat that supposedly gives Spaniards an "apariencia de maleantes e impide a las gentes civiles ver-les el rostro" (appearance of evildoers and prevents civil people from seeing their faces) (59–60). Nevertheless, he ends up adopting a Spanish saying, "Una buena capa todo lo tapa" (A good cape covers it all), and sends his servant, James, to hide beneath his cape several valuable stolen books from a monastery. In his letters, he describes himself and others according to the image he desires to portray; the discrepancy between the text and reality opens up a space of created images and suppressed identities.

Lord Aston-Howard's hypocrisy reaches its summit when he confronts a painting: "Trátese de un espléndido cuadro al óleo, . . . representando a una dama con su hijo, ambos ataviados con vestimenta española del siglo XVII. La factura, el estilo, el dominio del color y la delicadeza de la ejecución me in-clinan a pensar que su autor pudo ser el gran Velázquez, o en el peor de los casos uno de sus discípulos más diestros y aventajados" (It concerns a splen-did oil painting, . . . representing a lady with her son, both dressed in Spanish garments of the seventeenth century. The creation, the style, the dominion of the color, and the delicate execution make me inclined to think that the au-thor could have been the great Velázquez, or, in the worst of all cases, one of his most dexterous and advanced disciples) (78). Lord Aston-Howard's first desire is to possess this painting. But the canvas, inherited by the family that he is staying with in Spain, begins to possess him. The woman in the painting, identified as Doña Gracia de Mendoza, comes from noble lineage, a descen-dent, says the family, of the last Gothic king and of "linajes nobles, hidalgos limpios de sangre y otras ordinarieces de las que sólo hablan con tanto entusiasmo quienes acaban de adquirirlas" (noble lineages, noblemen clean of blood and other commonalities of which only those people who have acquired them speak about) (81).[7] Lord Aston-Howard finds himself seduced by the image of this woman. He suffers for her, he commits imaginary adultery with her, he becomes assaulted with "una cruel y dulcísima excitación" (a cruel and sweet excitement) (83) when he thinks that he might be sleeping in the same bedroom as she once did. He hardly finds rest, he cannot forget her delicate face, and he lets himself be captivated by a woman who does not exist (84). He becomes a hermit in the library of the house and finds out that, apart from her extreme beauty, she—not her dead husband—was very well educated in various languages and literary genres.

The feelings that this woman arouses in him make Lord Aston-Howard newly appreciate the country that he is visiting. His interest is now piqued by this "maja vestida" (clothed maja) that calls to mind Goya's seductive "maja desnuda" (nude maja) in a 1994 ad for Spanish tourism. The ad provokes foreigners (like Lord Aston-Howard) to indulge in Spain's treasures. Its headline, "Playmate 1798," resignifies the paintings of nude women that hang on the walls of Spain's museums and aristocratic households—like the one of Gracia de Mendoza. Goya's image is transformed into an erotic parody of a *Playboy* magazine centerfold. The woman depicted in the ad is said to get up from the canvas or the paper—Lord-Aston Howard's dream come true—and seduce Spain's tourists: "Si para admirar bellezas como ésta no se conforma con las coloridas páginas de una revista, anímese a verlas personalmente. Venga a los museos de España y encuéntrese cara a cara con estas obras como alguna vez lo hicieron Goya, Velázquez, Picasso, El Greco, Murillo, Dalí, El Bosco, Rubens, Miró, Sorolla. Bajo nuestro sol también tendrá mucho para disfrutar en la sombra" (If you do not want to resign yourself to admiring beauties on the colorful pages of a magazine, dare to see them for yourself. Come to the museums of Spain and find yourself face to face with these works as seen in their day by Goya, Velázquez, Picasso, El Greco, Murillo, Dalí, El Bosco, Rubens, Miró, and Sorolla. Under our sun you will also have much to enjoy in the shade). The large reproduction of Goya's painting, the bold-faced type announcing "Playmate 1798," and "España. Todo bajo el sol" (Spain: Everything under the sun), create a visual that stimulates its viewers' erotic dreams. In a similar manner, the portrait of Doña Gracia de Mendoza (or is it, as the academic said, Doña Rufina?) represents the inexpressible desire that Lord Aston-Howard feels for the female figure. In his internalized desire, he finds the perfect substitute for his innermost pleasures and horrors. I say "horrors" because when he sees Pepita, the daughter of his host family, and is confronted with the same eyes and features of the woman in the painting, the real playmate comes to life in the form of a young girl who reminds the lord of his own daughter.

As Lord Aston-Howard compares Pepita (Doña Gracia/Goya's "maja"/Spain's playmates) to his own daughter, he is unconsciously filled with incestuous feelings. She evokes in him the prohibited emotions that the painting had already projected in the third chapter. It is only when another man possesses—purchases—his hidden treasure that the painting loses its charm and breaks into pieces: "irrumpí en la dicha alcoba. El cuadro que allí encontré no es para describirlo a una dama, pero baste decir que pude ver a mi admirada doña Pepita, la deliciosa e ingenua niña que os había descrito, en la actitud más indecente que imaginarse pueda; mas mi sorpresa fue mayor cuando vi que el que compartía con ella esa vergonzosa situación no era otro que James, ese criado traidor en quien durante tanto tiempo puse mi confianza" (I burst into the said bedroom. The picture that I found there is not one that I can describe to a lady, but suffice it to say that I could see my admired Doña Pepita, the delicious and naive girl that I had described to you, in the most indecent position that one can imagine; but my surprise was surmounted when I saw that the one sharing this shameless situation was no other than James, this traitor servant in whom I had placed my trust for such a long time) (103).

Lord Aston-Howard substitutes one painting for another; he projects his pleasures, fantasies, and horrors onto a scene that, as it shatters, takes his desires with it. The painting provokes a total subversion of the visual and the textual into something that has been internalized. The hypocrisy of his words when he describes Pepita as a "naive child" foregrounds his manipulation of language throughout the chapter to create a distorted image of himself. The lord changes his image, "something like an actor on the historical stage, . . . from creatures 'made in the image' of the creator, to creatures who make themselves and their world in their own image" (Mitchell, *Reconfigured* 9). When the impact of the visual obliges him to disclose his disappointment textually, he abandons the painting and returns to his own textually constructed version of a truth designed to substitute for his shattered dreams. Pepita, the woman he desires, now becomes the "desvergonzada jovencita" (shameless young woman) (104) whose parents must be told about her indecent behavior and must be sent back to the convent. Since he cannot possess her, he must exert his linguistic power over her. In a letter to his wife, he conceals the truth about his disappointment by commenting on Spanish women's hypocrisy for hiding beneath a cape of religious virtuosity. Yet while his letters display his self-defined version of the truth, the palimpsest picture of Doña Gracia,

Pepita, and his own daughter when he sees her and is attracted to her upon his return to England discloses the power that the visual female image has in denying Lord Aston-Howard the pleasure of *having at a distance.*

The first chapter, most removed from the initial moment of investigation, takes place during the seventeenth century, the era of the Inquisition and visual control. Within the narrative spotlight of this time is an orphan boy, Pablito, who wanders from master to master. At the age of twelve, alone on the streets of Seville, he is begging in front of the theater when Doña Gracia de Mendoza notices him. She not only invites him into the theater to watch the piece, but she also takes him home as her servant. From the beginning (admiring her foot in the theater), Pablito falls in love with her, but he finds out that she, the woman who possesses his heart, is Jewish and "debía su próspera fortuna a la venta de las gracias que el mismo cielo le había dado y a la concesión de favores que a todos dispensaba" (owed her prosperous fortune to the sale of charms granted to her by the heavens and to the concession of favors that she bestowed on all) (37). After a group of men laugh at and beat up Pablito for being a prostitute's servant, Doña Gracia realizes the meaning of his pain: he is in love with her. At this point, Doña Gracia introduces Pablito to manhood, and their relationship blooms into full-fledged love, a love that, as the readers figure out later, may very well be incestuous, though unbeknownst to those involved.

Pablito is fifteen years old and Doña Gracia is thirty when they accept a wedding gift: a portrait painting by Zaide, a former slave who learned to paint in secret by observing his master. Because of his talent, Zaide is pardoned and set free by the king.[8] He paints the couple in such a realistic manner that Pablito says, "no semeja retrato, sino espejo verdadero y de él no nos diferenciamos sino en el hablar" (it does not resemble a portrait but a true mirror, and from it we do not differentiate ourselves but in speech) (50). The visual has become the truest version of reality; it is like a mirror, like a deformed, reversed image of the same coin. Nevertheless, the translation of a mimetic representation, according to Keith Moxey, "can never be precise. Much of our fascination with mimesis depends on the impossibility of translation. The artist always offers us that which the eye cannot see" (90). The painting in the first chapter is the *Urkunde.* Nevertheless, the visual has already been erased, and what the reader is confronted with are words on a page that describe a (misleading) moment of perfect mimesis. The letters act like a lure for the eye as the mind tries to translate them back into a visual representation. The process is multifold—from image to viewer, from viewer to writer, from writer to reader, from reader to imaginary viewer—and it ironically points to an inherent scotomatic relationship.

The mimetic representation of Pablito and Doña Gracia displaces the referent from its signifier and occludes its origin from the eyes of the Inquisition and its public. By placing their own bodies in public view, husband and wife displace the power of the Inquisition to name them "Jewish" or "prostitute" and instead define themselves. They erase those categories that would inscribe them into public and *published* figures. As "accused," they would be obliged by the Inquisition to wear signs around their necks with their names clearly written at the top; they would not be allowed to wear clothes made of silk, wear jewels, or carry swords (Alcalá 178). Instead of hiding their origin and their profession, they place themselves into the limelight by dressing and representing themselves in clothes made of silk and lace and by wearing jewels. A seventeenth- or a twentieth-century viewer does not see in the painting a Jewish prostitute marked by the Inquisition, but a person whose nobility allows her to openly express herself.

The image, as a mode of codification, inscribes the body with another's system of signification and exchanges one cultural meaning for another. The beholder is confronted with a creation that, as Pablito says, can be differentiated from the real image of himself only through speech, yet every act of speech is an act that creates new, deferred versions and takes the readers into deeper fictitious natures. Language automatically evokes difference. The painting now has the power to play with the beholder's visual expectations and to allow itself to be reinscribed with a new set of values. In a sense, it blinds the eyes of the Inquisition by determining its own site. Signification is displaced from the subject to the beholder. The image takes "truth" by the hand and molds it through "error."

The blind maiden has reached the river of History, the river that flows, changes, and disrupts significations as it travels downstream. The little pebbles that the old man places with much esteem in his pouch are those that form and transform history, specifically the narrative of a painting that travels through four generations of visions, versions, and significations. The irony that is brought to light within each chapter through the interplay of the visual and the textual, the constantly new fictitious aberration of "truth" that moves from a supposedly "objective" discovery to an ever more internalized version until it becomes its mirror image, reflects Shoshana Felman's idea that "each is . . . a potential threat to the interiority of the other, since each is contained in the other as its otherness-to-itself, its unconscious. As the unconscious traverses consciousness a theoretical body of thought always is traversed by its own unconsciousness, its own unthought, of which it is not aware, but which it contains in itself as the very conditions of its disruption, as the possibility of its own self-subversion" (10).

By undermining the scientific discourse in the fifth chapter, the visual disrupts the textual and sets up a series of deferred versions and aberrations of unconscious thoughts that suggest an *Urkunde* as that which "fluctuates according to those who see it: it can never be plumbed, once and for all" (Forster 17). Doña Gracia's body becomes the originary sight (literally) of inscription and unconscious desires based on a visuality that is translated into language. It is there that the visual and the textual point to a "thunderous collision between different worlds, destined to create, in and from the conflict between them, the new world that is the work" (Forster 13). When *El sueño* is read from the fifth chapter to the first, its characteristically postmodern, metanarrative irony highlights the deceiving power of the visual and the textual and points to the awareness of an always incomplete artificiality.

The inclusion of visual systems of signification questions textual authority. The narrative, on the other hand, includes a revision of the visual as a necessary site of parodic intentions. The manipulation of the image in each chapter is not perceived by the characters, who cannot see the changes applied to the painting between one period and another. The painting is, by implication, a parody of digital technology, which can transform images without apparent breaks. Manipulation is easy and rapid; it is unnoticeable to the naked eye, which cannot see the intermediate stage between capturing the image and printing it. The novel plays with the idea of image correction as something that becomes increasingly elastic. Images are not so much about original creations as they are about "giving meaning and value to computational ready-mades by appropriation, transformation, reprocessing and recombination" (Mitchell, *Reconfigured* 7). The inclusion of the visual in *El sueño* does not represent a simple mimetic analysis of images but a turn toward the pictorial that reflects

> a postlinguistic, postsemiotic rediscovery of the picture as a complex interplay between visuality, apparatus, institutions, discourse, bodies, figurality. It is the realization that *spectatorship* (the look, the gaze, the glance, the practices of observation, surveillance, and visual pleasure) may be as deep a problem as various forms of *reading* (decipherment, decoding, interpretation, etc.) and that visual experience or "visual literacy" might not be fully explicable on the model of textuality. (Mitchell, *Picture* 16)

As this passage suggests, the visual is as complex a site of significations as the textual. In Díaz-Mas's novel, the image must be analyzed next to and in reference to the text in order to produce a critical exercise of visual literacy or literary visuality. Specifically, the novel suggests that renewed interest be paid to the (re-)creation of the female body as an erotically charged image used to promote everything, from a product (a book) to a voice (an author).

Notes

1. It is interesting to note that in the United States three novels have recently appeared on the *New York Times* best-seller list that echo the task presented by Díaz-Mas several years earlier: *Girl in Hyacinth Blue* (1999) by Susan Vreeland, *The Music Lesson* (1999) by Katharine Weber, and *Girl with a Pearl Earring* (2001) by Tracy Chevalier.

2. Díaz-Mas has claimed, "'Está todo dentro de esa línea de la metaficción historiográfica que no pretende ser novela histórica en el sentido de que no pretende reconstruir la historia ni reconstruir exactamente épocas históricas, sino presentar esas épocas históricas como metáfora de algo'" (It all pertains to this line of historiographic metafiction that does not pretend to be a historical novel in the sense that it does not pretend to reconstruct history or exactly reconstruct historical periods, but to introduce the historical epochs as metaphors of something) (qtd. in Ferrán 328). This "algo" is what I claim is the power of the visual image in the late twentieth century.

3. Throughout the novel, the narrator alludes to parodic recreations of literary genres (see Glenn 483–90).

4. Díaz-Mas explains that this chapter is based on her own experience:

> Lo curioso es que aquello del cuadro en mi novela es una anécdota real, y además bastante divertida. Cuando yo era pequeña, mis padres tenían por el salón una mesa bastante fea. Yo me tumbaba en el suelo, miraba la parte de abajo de la mesa y veía unos ojos que me miraban y me daban auténtico pánico. Le decía a mi madre que allí habían unos ojos, y mi madre me decía lo mismo que le dice la madre a la niña en la novela: "no, no, eso serán los nudos de la madera". En efecto, era una cara, ¡y la cara de Franco! Luego me enteré, años después, de que mi abuelo había tenido un bar. Cuando acabó la guerra obligaron en todos los establecimientos públicos a poner un gran retrato de Franco, de madera. Luego, cuando se quitó la obligación de tener ese retrato, un empleado del bar con la madera de aquel retrato hizo una mesa. Así que los ojos malos aquellos que aparecen eran en realidad del retrato de Franco. (qtd. in Ferrán 332–33)

> [What is curious is that the painting in my novel is based on a real anecdote and, moreover, is very funny. When I was little, my parents had a rather ugly table in the living room. I used to lie on the floor, look at the underside of the table, and see a pair of eyes that looked at me and produced in me an authentic sense of panic. I told my mother that there was a pair of eyes, and my mother told me the same thing that the mother tells the child in the novel: "no, those must be the knots in the wood." In effect, it was a face, and the face of Franco! Later I found out, years later, that my grandfather had owned a bar. When the war ended they obliged all public establishments to hang up a large, wooden, portrait of Franco. Later, when the obligation was lifted, an employee of the bar used the wood of that portrait to build a table. Therefore, the evil eyes that appear were in reality a portrait of Franco].

5. The "Sección Femenina" was the women's section of the Spanish Fascist party. Founded in 1934, it was part of the state body. It "was charged with the socialization and control of Spanish female youth and womanhood in accordance with the ideology of

the new regime. In particular, it ran a form of labour service for unmarried women (compulsory for nearly all working women) through which the regime achieved rudimentary social services virtually gratis" (Graham and Labanyi 424)

6. Lord Aston-Howard is a historical figure. His character refers to the well-known Lord High Admiral of England, in charge of the Royal Navy, who attacked Cádiz and visited Valladolid in the sixteenth century (Johnson, "La española" 388). I would like to thank María Antonia Garcés for this and other historical information in this chapter.

7. The name Gracia brings to mind Gracia de Alfarache, the wife of Guzmán in *Guzmán de Alfarache* by Mateo Alemán.

8. The character Zaide is a historical reference to Juan de Pareja, a slave of Velázquez's, who was freed in Rome on 23 November 1650 precisely for the same reasons as described in *El Sueño* (see Brown, *Velázquez* 201). In the picaresque tradition, Zaide also alludes to Lazarillo de Tormes's Moorish stepfather. The name Pablito echos Francisco de Quevedo's character Pablos in *Buscón* (1626).

2

The Art of Seduction:
Urraca by Lourdes Ortiz

From the feminist text *El rapto del Santo Grial* (The Abduction of the Holy Grail) by Paloma Díaz-Mas to the prizewinning novel *El hereje* (The Heretic) by Miguel Delibes and the best-selling series *El capitán Alatriste* (The Captain Alatriste) by Arturo Pérez Reverte, historical novels have become one of Spain's most popular genres. According to a survey from 1998, the historical novel accounts for 35.1 percent of preferred reading material within the contemporary narrative category (second to adventure novels at 37.3 percent) (*Informe* 122). While historical narratives have been successful for many decades, their popularity skyrocketed at the end of the twentieth century because of the use of attractive frameworks that combine the historical genre with the detective, adventure, or erotic genres. Their popularity, according to the author Ángeles de Irisarri, resides in the changing constituency of a readership that studies less history and searches for its roots "en parte en la divulgación que realizan este tipo de historias" (in part in the disclosure that these type of histories provide) (Irisarri n.p.).[1]

The space that is opened for re-creation and remembrance in historical texts is especially appealing to authors who desire to give voice to forgotten female figures and events. Mothers, daughters, wives, and lovers are reaffirmed in fictions by authors like Clara Obligado in *La hija de Marx* (The Daughter of Marx) (1996), Ángeles de Irisarri in *Isabel, la Reina* (Isabel, the Queen), Magdalena Lasala in *La estirpe de la mariposa* (The Heirs of the Butterfly), and Almudena de Arteaga del Alcázar in *La Beltraneja: el pecado oculto de Isabel la Católica* (The Beltraneja: The Hidden Sin of Isabel la Católica.[2] The protagonists of these writings usually conform to standards of noble women, with political ambition, know-how, personal strength, and intelligence, and a personality that is often referred to as "varonil" (manly).

Two novels, *La reina Urraca* (Queen Urraca) (2000) by Ángeles de Irisarri and *La princesa de Éboli* (The Princess of Éboli) (1998) by Almudena de Arteaga del Alcázar, are reminiscent of *Urraca* by Lourdes Ortiz, the book studied in this chapter. While the first novel mirrors the content of *Urraca* (first published by Puntual in 1982 and later by Debate in 1991 and 1995), the second follows its structure.[3] On a black and red ribbon that wraps the 2001 edition of *La princesa de Éboli,* Luis María Ansón, a member of the Real Academia Española de la Lengua, states that the novel is the "Crónica de un crimen de estado, una historia de amor magníficamente descrita... Se lee de un tirón" (chronicle of a state crime, a magnificently written love story. . . . It can be read in one sitting). In bold, capital letters, the ribbon attempts to increase the book's value by highlighting that the novel is in its nineteenth edition. While this claim lacks authority if readers know that an edition usually comprises one thousand to five thousand copies, it does serve to attract an audience in search of a disguised best-seller.

The cover of the novel represents a painting of the Princess of Éboli (fig. 4) by the Spanish painter Alonso Sánchez Coello (1531–88). In small, italicized type below the image, the book publishers claim the princess is "La mujer más enigmática y fascinante del Siglo de Oro" (the most enigmatic and fascinating woman of the Golden Age). Peeking out from behind this suggestive ribbon, readers encounter her gaze, though one of her eyes is hidden behind a patch. The enigmatic character of this woman, Ana de Mendoza, derives from when, at an early age, she lost an eye during either a fall or a fencing duel (the historical origin of her accident is not verified). As was the case in *El sueño de Venecia,* in which the blind maiden was accompanied by Error, this fiction provides a visual referent for the historical as a hybrid form between the seen and the unseen. The patch demonstrates readers' inability to separate the real from the fictitious and true from false. The image of the Princess of Éboli serves as a metaphor for the practices of the historical novel: the blurring of truth, the omission or recasting of information, and the reading of "high" literature with a touch of best-seller.

Urraca seduces the readers by interweaving erotically charged tales and historical data to produce an account of a forgotten female figure, Queen Urraca. Historical texts explain that Queen Urraca was the daughter of Alfonso VI and Constanza of Burgundy and the wife of Raimundo of Burgundy. She gave birth to Alfonso VII and a daughter. Upon the death of her husband and father, Queen Urraca ascended to the throne and married Alfonso I, the king

Figure 4.   Book cover of *La princesa de Éboli* by Almudena de Arteaga
del Alcázar (1998) with painting of the princess of Éboli by Alonso
Sánchez Coello. (Reprinted with the permission of Ediciones Martínez
Roca, S.A.)

of Aragon and the heir to a family that had conquered Moorish territory in
Spain and France since 1035. Queen Urraca ruled amid conspiracy and strife
between 1109 and 1126 and was imprisoned in the monastery Valcabados in
1123 by her son. Ortiz's book begins in 1123, during Urraca's residence behind
stone walls, and it (supposedly) ends in 1126, the year of her death.

Ortiz plays with the readers in a similar manner as the image on the book cover of *La princesa de Éboli* seduces its viewers. The author presents her queen through the first-person narrative of an imprisoned woman who has been pushed out of the political arena, and history, by her son. Confined, Urraca decides to take another look at herself by telling a monk, Roberto, the story of her political life. Through the art of storytelling, Urraca attempts to reinsert herself into the history from which she has been expatriated, pushed out, and written over as queen and as woman. For her story, or product, to gain value and be heard or bought, Urraca depends on her powers of invention, on her ability to spin plots; manipulate words, bodies, and events; and include her fantasies, legends, and utopias into the making of a new story. In order to do this, she cuts her story—or inserts blind spots—by metaphorically taking a pair of scissors and eliminating sections of her narrative, thus playing with elisions, pauses, and silences. At the same time, she inserts sexually charged scenes where objective history should abide. The mechanism of the cut allows her to open up the space between characters and events and glue the parts back together in her own voice. Urraca places her body at the center of the text and plays with forces that can increase the seductive quality of her present, yet absent, female figure. By using the cut as a device to propel the narrative and by emphasizing her central position in history, Urraca turns herself into a product—she attempts to sell herself—and increases the desire she arouses in others through techniques that emulate those used in the advertising industry.

The world of the image is not foreign to Lourdes Ortiz, who at present resides in Madrid, directs the Real Escuela Superior de Arte Dramático, and teaches art history classes. Ortiz has dedicated much of her life to the study of the plastic arts, which, she says, have taught her many things about the relationship between form and content (Porter 140). Ortiz has worked in a wide range of genres and has applied a variety of artistic and cinematic techniques in each case. In an interview with Lynn McGovern, the author states:

> En mi primera novela, *Luz de memoria,* cuento con elementos cinematográficos, escenas que están trabajadas un poco como un guión. A veces hay momentos de flashback, que pueden ser cinematográficos. Supongo que está en lo que he intentado crear en *En días como éstos,* que es una novela muy corta, con estructura de guión. De una forma he intentado contar algo que vosotros, los anglosajones, domináis muy bien: la acción, un relato en el que casi no hay diálogos, ni adjetivos. Además hay otro elemento: a veces los personajes son caricaturas, son plásticos, esto imita la pintura. (McGovern, "Lourdes" 48)

[In my first novel, *Luz de memoria* (Light of Memory), I count on cinematic elements, scenes that are worked similar to that of a screenplay. Sometimes there are flashbacks that can be cinematic. I guess I tried to do this in *En días como éstos* (In Days Like These), which is a short novel structured like a screenplay. In some manner, I try to do what you Anglo-Saxons dominate very well: action, a story in which there is almost no dialogue or adjectives. There is also another element: sometimes the characters are caricatures, they are plastic. This imitates painting].

Ortiz claims that *Arcángeles* (Archangels) is one of her most plastic works because each chapter represents a painting. The text begins with Fra Angelico's *Annunciation* and ends with Michelangelo's *Final Judgement*. The narrative moves from a medieval, angelical picture to a disrupted one from the Renaissance. Ortiz says that, in general, her work is filled with images, "tanto en *Arcángeles* como en mi última novela, *Antes de la batalla*. Todo se cuenta a través de la imagen" (in *Arcángeles* as well as in my latest novel, *Antes de la batalla* (Before the Battle), everything is told through the image) (McGovern, "Lourdes" 48).

Urraca is one of Ortiz's least plastic but most suggestively visual novels. The book gained attention in the North American academy mostly because of its feminist revision of history. It joins historicity with a pronounced feminist approach that attempts to reinsert women into the written framework. Lynn McGovern analyzes the novel in relation to Linda Hutcheon's concept of "historiographic metafiction." Lynn Talbot discusses how "Urraca . . . illuminates the way historical fiction can accomplish three purposes: question the accuracy of historical accounts, establish a new consciousness about the relationship between women and power, and redefine the concept of hero" (438). Nina Molinaro interprets the text within a Foucaultian framework to demonstrate its fascination with "the centripetal pull of political authority and feminine sexual desire" ("Simulacra" 47). Biruté Ciplijauskaité, like Carmen Rivera Villegas, views the novel as a voyage of self-discovery, and Lilit Thwaites compares *Urraca* to Antonio Gala's play *Anillos para una dama* (Rings for a Lady) to point to the protagonists' freedom of choice.

Elizabeth Ordóñez and Robert Spires are two scholars who have most extensively interpreted the novel's sexual dimension. Spires states that Urraca finds in political and physical pleasure only temporary relief and discovers that the play of language offers her longer-lasting, more satisfying experiences. He denominates this dimension of the queen's games as "the joys of textual stimulation" (135). This "joy" turns the text into a metaerotic novel, one that not only works with seduction on the level of content but works on the level of language as well. Ordóñez believes that the entire novel centers on the

theme of passion as erotic excitement, bellicose exhilaration, or religious ecstasy: "These three passions often overlap as the bed is recalled a battleground
of aphrodisiac sin, a den of conspiracy; the battleground is remembered as the
dust and sweat perfumed boudoir of the queen's love of empire; the church
is evoked as the bishop's bedroom and the planning chamber for intrigue and
the satisfaction of his lust for power" (*Voices* 142). My own reading of *Urraca*
is based on the insights presented by Ordóñez and Spires as well as on the
power of the female body and the body of narrative as marketable products.
The subversive quality of the narrative lies in Urraca's ability to play with the
visual and verbal power of her "body" as a site of seduction-as-disappearance.

As a product sold in the Spanish market of the 1980s and 1990s, a market
that increasingly uses nude images and seductive book covers, it is curious that
Urraca was never promoted as an erotic-historical novel—one whose erotic
component propels the narrative's historical specificity. The few book reviews
published about the text point to the testimonial and feminist dimensions of
the narrative and describe the novel as a historical text. The 1991 Debate edition and its not particularly erotic book cover do not pique readers' sexual curiosity. In fact, the cover depicts two not very romantic, humanized chairs (fig.
5). The chair on the right appears to be a hard, wooden seat depicting a devil
or a man in black who may remind readers of the "desconocido vestido de
negro" (unknown person dressed in black) in Carmen Martín Gaite's *El cuarto
de atrás* (The Back Room). The chair on the left appears comfortable and represents a fluffy female figure with curtainlike qualities. The theatrical backdrop displays a slit in the material through which various unidentified objects
bulge onto a stage of red tiles. There is nothing that could be interpreted as remotely sexual on either the front or the back cover of the book, where the plot
is described as one filled with loneliness, love, and power in medieval Spain,
a story of one as well as many women.

Upon opening the book, readers are immediately pulled into a story that
uses one of the oldest tricks in the trade. The very first paragraph ends with:
"Nadie debe, ni puede compadecer a Urraca. Todavía no estoy vencida..." (Nobody should or can feel sorry for Urraca. I am not yet defeated—) (9). Similar to the blind spots in *El sueño de Venecia,* those that shadow truth through
vision, this statement fills the scene with mysterious apprehension. The female
narrator demands attention from her readers, who are intrigued to fill in the
space between the suspension points and who are pulled into the making of
a female figure who is about to sell them a story.

The success of Urraca's tale depends on the production of her story as a site
of textual and sexual consumption. Her technique functions similarly to that
used in advertising, which relies on the imaginary desire that mostly visual

Figure 5.   Book cover of *Urraca* by Lourdes Ortiz (1991). (Designed by José Crespo; illustration by Claude Verlinde, *Les fauteuils,* 1979; reprinted with the permission of Editorial Debate)

referents produce in its audience. In both advertising and narrative, hundreds of individually created "appeals" are employed to convey messages. An appeal in advertising "refers to the basis or approach used . . . to elicit some consumer response or to influence consumer feelings toward the product, service, or cause" (Belch and Belch 478). In narrative, an appeal may be equated to the power that its content and technique have in conveying the author's message successfully. Some advertising approaches may be directly translated into literary genres such as the testimonial, "whereby a person speaks on behalf of the product or service based on his or her personal use of and/or experiences with it"; the fantastic, "where a commercial can become a 30-second escape for the viewer into the realm or lifestyle"; or dramatization, "where the focus is on telling a short story with the product or service as the star or hero [and often relying on the problem/solution approach]" (ibid. 494–95). Other approaches, such as humor, comparison, slice of life, or personality symbol may be found in any particular text. Santos Zunzunegui believes that advertising comprises a narrative space that represents actions and passions, gestures, looks, behaviors, and judgments. At stake is not so much the object to desire but "mostrar el deseo en acto. Sólo así, deseando el deseo del otro, podrá encontrar un espacio de maniobra el interlocutor implícito que todo anuncio reclama" (presenting the act of desire itself. Only this way, by desiring the desire of an other, can the implicit interlocutor of any ad claim a space to maneuver) (14).

In 1982, when *Urraca* was first published, the cultural industry was becoming well aware of the importance of promotional media to a text's success. While one certainly cannot claim that Ortiz consciously used advertising techniques in the construction of her novel, it does seem possible that she was aware of the visual power of the erotic female body in the construction of womanhood, especially during the sexually liberating post-Franco period— "el destape"—when nude images flooded the streets of Spain. It may come as no surprise, then, that Urraca promotes herself as History through the hidden delights that her body and her body of narrative have to offer.

Readers of *Urraca* learn that the queen has been objectified and nullified by the Catholic church, which sides with her son and denounces her as a murderer and an adulterous queen. Urraca's task is to convince the public that *her* version of her political past, not their version, is true. The only way that Urraca can fulfill this task is by infusing desire into herself as object. She must turn herself into a product to be desired (place herself on the cover of her own book) for her readers to feel interpellated and thus metamorphosed by the vision that envelops them. Urraca's listener and viewer is the monk Roberto, who visits her in her cell on a daily basis. Roberto's religious vows give Urraca an added tool: she uses his innocence as an excuse to cut him—and the readers—off from the telling of erotic tales and to tease him and the readers with random pieces of a puzzle. She approaches this task by interrupting the narrative flow with constant excuses. The first one concerns the effect that Roberto's body has on her: "No, todavía no voy a hablarte del conde. Estoy algo cansada y esta ternura que me producen tus cabellos despeinados, . . . se parece demasiado al deseo" (No, I am not yet going to tell you about the count. I am a bit tired and this tenderness that your uncombed hair produces in me . . . reminds me too much of desire) (34). She formulates another excuse by telling Roberto that she needs to adhere to the format of a chronicle, defined as "a detailed and continuous record of events in order of time; a historical record in which facts are related [usually] without interpretation" (Brown, *Oxford* 397). Therefore, she claims, "no voy a narrar la risa a destiempo de don Pedro, su carcajada de gozador, sus mejillas rojas, ni te voy a hablar de la ternura de Gómez González, de su fidelidad, de su delicadeza. Esos, monje, no son temas para una crónica" (I am not going to narrate the inopportune laugh of Don Pedro, nor am I going to tell you about the tenderness of Gómez González, of his fidelity, of his sensitivity. Those, monk, are no topics for a chronicle) (43). Urraca plays the monk to divert attention from one character or topic of conversation to another: "le cuento al monje y él, como si no quisiera saber, como si presintiese las cosas que no deben ser dichas, pregunta por don Pedro." (I tell the monk and he, as if he did not want to know, as if he could sense the things that should not be said, asks about Don Pedro) (44). She also plays him in order to indulge in the sexual fantasies of others. She smoothly inserts the monk in the position of her characters, increases his sexual appetite, and slowly pulls him into the erotic narrative energy of her advertisement. She compares his hands, destined to caress her skin, to those of Aben Ammar, one of her husband's Moorish warriors (33); she linguistically maneuvers Roberto into one of Zaida's—her father's lover's—rooms filled with silk cushions. Here she asks him to imagine lying down on the bed and to enjoy the feeling of Urraca's tongue on his body and her playing of the lute (34). The queen uses conditional verbs—"podrías recostarte" (you could lie back) or "yo tocaría para ti"(I would play for you)— to include Roberto in her past sexual life and to awaken his imagination to the possibility of a future encounter. The irony of her comparison with Zaida, who is nothing like the Urraca the readers come to know, discloses her amorous intentions, flights into fantasy, and linguistic manipulations. Urraca's talent of constantly shifting the subject-object positions between the characters of her tale and her listener, Roberto, discloses her understanding that a great text and a great ad must be, by definition, erotic. Hence, Roland Barthes's proclamation: "The text you write must prove to me that it desires me" (6).

Queen Urraca's narration unveils the ability with which the clothed or un-dressed female body—its teasing capacity—can market her tale. History and sexuality move into new venues of production as Urraca discloses her and her compatriots' ability to manipulate both, which, like the task of medieval trou-badours, is based precisely on the ability to influence readers' emotional reac-tions to a story through gestures, tone, and suspense. She applies her own body less to baring her beauty or gaining sexual gratification than to indulging in the act of seducing her public through words. Seduction becomes her prime ve-hicle for rewriting history because, as Jean Baudrillard points out, in the fem-inine lies "the privilege of having never acceded to truth or meaning, and of having remained absolute master of the realm of appearances. The capacity im-manent to seduction to deny things their truth and turn it into a game, the pure play of appearances, and thereby foil all systems of power and meaning with a mere turn of the hand. The ability to turn appearances in on themselves, to play on the body's appearances, rather than with the depths of desire" (*Seduction* 8).

Urraca's historical and narrative power depends on her ability to wield the sword as well as she wields the pen and to play with the strings of her corset as well as she strings together words. The queen, for example, in reaction to losing a duel to a young squire, demonstrates how she uses her sexuality to overpower her opponents: "fingí cansancio y, mientras reculaba, dejé que se abrieran las cintas de mi corpiño. Allí, ante la mirada del escudero, mis dos pechos saltaban; nuevo e inesperado, el cuerpo de Urraca parecía ofrecérsele. Guzmán vaciló, y yo coloqué la punta de mi espada en su nuez que se agitaba cada vez más deprisa" (I feigned exhaustion and, while I retreated, I let the ribbons of my bodice open. There, before the eyes of the squire, my two breasts jumped; new and unexpectantly the body of Urraca seemed to offer itself to him. Guzmán hesitated, and I placed the point of my sword on his Adam's apple, which shook faster by the moment) (19). The queen allows the squire, and the readers, to peek at the most intimate details of her (political) life. Se-duction is the act that allows for a reconstructed (and regendered) discourse to come into play and gain value.

The techniques that Urraca uses to seduce her opponents work in a simi-lar manner on a narrative level. Urraca does not hide her mechanisms. She openly explains that in order to describe the silence of her mother, Constanza, she uses "puntos suspensivos, que dejan eco para que enraíce la duda" (sus-pension points, which allow doubt to take root) (86), and she applies Con-stanza's art of storytelling to change voices and pause "en los momentos cul-minantes para despertar la expectativa y la tensión" (during the culminating moments to awaken expectation and tension) (81). She also highlights the power of adjectives and the rhythmic succession of verbs, and the way she plays and mixes letters, because "el deseo, yo lo sé, para que no se agote, requiere la construcción, el invento" (desire, I know, requires construction and invention for it not to be exhausted) (111). She uses the obscene and the forbidden to increase her readers' desire, and she piques her readers' curiosity by writing about events outside socially acceptable sexual behavior. Urraca pushes the historical beyond its limits when she mentions her husband's homosexual desires and fancy for menstrual blood, her father's incestuous tendencies and adulterous acts with Moorish girls, the bishop's delight in hearing about "sayas levantadas" (lifted skirts) (29), and Raimundo's obsession with young girls. She talks about Al-Mutamid, the king of Seville, and his enchantment with "niños rubios y morenos, que se dejaban recorrer como si fueran miel que puede ser libada" (blond- and black-haired boys who let themselves be caressed as if they were honey to be sipped) (33), and she points to Roberto's desire to break his religious vows.[4] She makes the readers aware that she is painting a unique portrait and that she is consciously constructing a product that has an audience and a figure that is heard, told, and, most importantly, sold.

The monk's role in Urraca's story becomes most apparent when he finally succumbs to her "textual stimulations," as so succinctly described by Spires (135), and has sexual intercourse with the queen. The readers find that, more than a source of pleasure for Urraca, the act serves to enhance the visual quality of her discourse: "Bien; por fin ha sucedido. No ha sido demasiado gratificante, pero me ha traído la calma. La carne blanca y sin vello de mi monje me ha traído la huella de otros cuerpos... cuerpos que se dejan, se tocan, se olvidan, cuerpos que regresan como vapores, trayendo olores, tactos" (Good, at last it has happened. It was not extremely gratifying but it brought me calm. The white and hairless skin of my monk has brought me the mark of other bodies—bodies that yielded, that touched, that forgot, bodies that return like vapors, bringing smells, touches) (117). Roberto's corporal presence (and his physical absence in chapter 14, the only chapter in which he is not present) propels an endless repetition of memories that lack fixed signifiers and permit Urraca to indulge in a multiplicity of stories. The substitution of one body for another and subsequently the body for the word—"como no hay cuello que acariciar, ni muslos que recorrer, hablo en voz alta" (since there is no neck to caress, no thighs to peruse, I speak in a loud voice) (131)—are logical if readers consider that Urraca has been extrapolated from time, space, and agency and placed in a prison cell far away from the making of history. Taken out of the actual turn of events, she positions herself within a parenthesis where, "hasta el hermano Roberto . . . es ya parte del texto que tengo que contar; ya no vivo su carne, sino en tanto que crónica" (even brother Roberto . . . is already part of the text that I have to tell: no more do I live for his flesh, but as chronicle) (119). Urraca makes history without being part of history. Her first-person narrative is how she can relive, reorder, and understand the past and rewrite the future.

Urraca's promotional powers appear successful when Roberto is asked to change positions with the queen and finish her chronicle. Urraca asks him to be part of an interactive project whereby her biography would mix with his narrative abilities and his religious authority: "quisiera yo, Roberto, que tú completaras mi crónica, introduciendo la metáfora, jugando con las palabras" (I would like you, Roberto, to complete my chronicle, introducing the metaphor, playing with the words) (193). When she turns the tables and allows him to include his fantasies in the making of the story, Urraca becomes the monk's potential character, and he can then unclothe her and introduce her as a medium of seduction (if he so desires) into his own texts. Spires believes that, "although she ostensibly grants him poetic license, his creation will inevitably reveal the traces of hers. His male-centered discourse must respond to, and therefore can never totally erase, the female-centered discourse that inspired it. She has managed to transform a linguistic phenomenon into an aesthetic experience: the dual gender of the word *fe(male)*" (140). If one views the novel through the techniques that Urraca applies to seduce her readers and takes into account that by handing the text over to Roberto she also opens up the narrative to her future readers, one could say that Urraca's discourse is (fe)male from the very beginning. Interpreted on a metanarrative level, the final sexual encounter—"Déjate ir dentro de mí" (Let yourself go within me)—gives free rein to inclusion and immersion. All readers are invited to insert themselves into Urraca's picture and play with her textual body's various pleasures. This, perhaps, is Urraca's truest revenge. The readers, after finishing the last words of the text, take *Urraca* and Queen Urraca and incorporate them into their stories, memories, and articles in a manner similar to the academic in *El sueño de Venecia.*

The interactive attributes of Urraca's text are reminiscent of Baudrillard's definition of seduction as "an ironic alternative form, one that breaks the referentiality of sex and provides a space, not of desire, but of play and defiance" (*Seduction* 21). For Baudrillard, seduction does "not lead to fused or con-fused relations . . . but to dual relations. It is not a matter of a mystical fusion of subject or object, or signifier and signified, masculine and feminine, etc., but of a seduction, that is, a *duel and agonistic* relation" (ibid. 105). Oppositions do not simply merge and conveniently disappear in *Urraca;* they dance around one another and challenge one another's authority, thus playing with the *dual* nature of the duel. In Urraca's case, these duels are literal and metaphorical as she fights against squires, the church, Roberto's religious vows, history, and the linearity of the chronicle—and they are agonistic in the sense that her task is based on crafting visually effective arguments and propelling appeals.

The dual nature of Urraca's seduction is based on a series of edges, most importantly those that divide history from fiction, presence from absence, and telling from concealing information. These edges function like two lips sewn together to create a new discourse, but instead of fusing both elements into one—as many critics believe *Urraca* does in the realms of history and fiction, masculinity and femininity—the queen creates a narrative that cuts the two lips apart and discloses the limits and powers of both. In other words, she allows readers to identify both edges and therefore locate the holes between the lips into which they may metaphorically, or literally, in Roberto's case, introduce themselves. She unlocks the lips of women who have been silent and silenced for centuries, and she opens their lips to tales of sexual and textual pleasure. In effect, *Urraca* plays with Barthes's definition of pleasure as the creation of "Two edges . . . : an obedient, conformist, plagiarizing edge (the language is to be copied in its canonical state, as it has been established by schooling, good usage, literature, culture), and another edge, mobile, blank (ready to assume any contours) . . . the place where the death of language is glimpsed" (6). The "place where the death of language is glimpsed" is where Urraca creates a heightened erotic product of herself. This product is one in which linguistic referents are buried beneath the pleasure that their imaginary bodies promote.

The last paragraph of the novel, in which Urraca suggests that she poison herself, exemplifies how death—the absence of the protagonist or product—enhances Urraca's narrative seduction. The doubt in the readers' minds—they never learn whether she does commit suicide—exemplifies what Ortiz describes as "un intento irónico de que la muerte no sea vencedora, una especie de juego" (an ironic attempt to let death not be victorious, a kind of game) (qtd. in Morales Villena 10). The queen's suggested death plays with seduction as "an appearance-as-disappearance" (Barthes 10). Baudrillard believes that for a woman's act of seduction to be successful, "her entire character, all her feminine resources must be mobilized, and simultaneously suspended. It is not a question of surprising her in the passivity of her innonence; her freedom of action must be in play. Because it is by this freedom, by its movement—and the curves and sudden twists imparted to it by seduction—that she must, seemingly spontaneously, reach that point where, unbeknownst to herself, she will be lost" (107–8). Beknownst to herself, Queen Urraca is lost in history. She rewrites herself in a framework that includes *female* pleasure—

based on her gender—with female *pleasure*—based on textual and sexual enjoyment—in order to produce a uniquely seductive text. The narrative gives way to a series of frames that both disclose and conceal Urraca's actual historical story. The vignettes of the queen's life express her tale through many different "curves and sudden twists" (Baudrillard 107), only to portray a half-painted picture and impart a stronger feeling of loss.

Urraca becomes the absent force behind her own text because she is a figure whose representation has been written out of history, which gives her more creative space to write herself back into it. In other words, she becomes "the spectator who occupies the missing field as the 'Absent One'" (Silverman, *Threshold* 204). Her power resides in her disappearance. The "absent one," with its psychoanalytical undertones, is a figure who "has all the attributes of the mythically symbolic father: potency, knowledge, transcendental vision, self-sufficiency, and discursive power" (ibid.). The queen moves from being the abject other to being the all-powerful voice behind her own image, because, on a visual level, the text embodies her in only one form: the sculpture that stands in the church and defines her as an adulterer. This is an image filled with negative connotations while it also functions much like a modern-day advertisement: it promotes a behavior that, in this case, should not be followed. But Urraca notices bemusedly that her sculpture is located next to and is confused with Christ: "la Adúltera crece y se convierte en símbolo. . . . La Adúltera confirma mi triunfo. Cuando todos hayan olvidado a Urraca, mi relieve seguirá en pie, demonio encarnado; tú me has igualado al Altísimo, sin proponértelo, tu absurda broma me ha dado memoria" (the Adulteress grows and turns into a symbol. . . . The Adulteress confirms my triumph. When all have forgotten Urraca, my relief will remain standing, the devil embodied. Without intending to, you have equaled me to the Almighty. Your absurd joke has given me memory) (125). The novel opens up the representation of Urraca as a performance of pleasure that, in Silverman's words, "depends on the occlusion of the enunciatory point of view and the seeming boundlessness of the image" (*Threshold* 126). Because her sculpture is placed next to the figure of Christ, the promotional message of her figure is decontextualized and resignified as it moves from an adulterous wife to a religious deity, from Urraca to the voice of authority.

The sculpture of the queen is symbolic of a widespread imaginary power with which the female body arouses its readers and challenges the limits and powers of language. The prohibited figure of the female adulterer gives *Urraca* the visual edge that many erotic novels generously play with and count on to describe liberated (although not necessarily more female) scenes of woman's sexuality. The sculpture allows the text to work on the margins of the cognitive sign. The adulterous queen, created as a propagandistic medium of twelfth-century misbehavior, comes alive within a narrative that redefines the symbolic nature of the sculpture for twentieth-century readers as an example of sexual liberation. The sculpture serves as a visual, albeit ambiguous, conclusion to the path along which two time periods converge. Above all, the figure exemplifies the power that the erotic has in the creation of a new text in the eyes of its viewers. Urraca's dialogic monologue allows her to slip her own image back into the history that has forgotten her. She does so by metamorphosing the power of the very cuts that have cut her out. She appropriates the cut as a tool of seduction that breaks the barriers of correct historical writing, correct historical content, and reader expectations. Urraca becomes, to borrow Barthes's words, a "Text of bliss: [a] text that imposes a state of loss, [a] text that discomforts . . . , unsettles the reader's historical, cultural, psychological assumptions, the consistency of his [or her] tastes, values, memories, brings to a crisis his [or her] relation with language" (14). Urraca breaks down taboos and appropriates the limiting and objectifying characteristics of the female body to her advantage. She parodies the power of the product by making reference to the seductive quality of an image that is never fully seen. Urraca subverts authority by making the explicit (female body) implicit. She places her own body at the center of textual attention and propels stories of other bodies from it, including those of other female voices. More than as a sexual entity, her body serves as a metanarrative device that points to the manner in which she and, by extension, Spanish women writers play with language to seduce subjects and reposition the historically (and visually) fixed identity of women as products.

Notes

1. Other historical texts from the post-Franco period include *En busca del unicornio* by Juan Eslava, *El mal amor* by Fernando Fernán Gómez, *El insomnio de una noche de invierno* by Eduardo Alonso, *La vieja sirena* by José Luis Sampedro, *Mansura* by Félix de Azúa, *Extramuros* by Jesús Fernández Santos, *Babilonia, la puerta del cielo* by Andrés Sorel, and *La piedra del diablo* by Manuel Ayllón. See Langa Pizarro on historical novels of the twentieth century.

2. Other novels by these three female writers include *Moras y cristianas, Isabel, la Reina; El sabor de las cerezas; El viaje de la reina; La cajita de lágrimas; La reina Urraca;* and *Las damas del fin del Mundo* by Ángeles de Irisarri; *Moras y cristianas* (co-writer), *La estirpe de la mariposa, El círculo de los muchachos de blanco, Abderramán III,* and *Fábulas de ahora* by Magdalena Lasala, and *La Beltraneja. El pecado oculto de Isabel la Católica; La vida privada del emperador; Eugenia de Montijo;* and *La princesa de Éboli* by Almudena de Arteaga del Alcázar.

3. *La princesa de Éboli* follows the life of Ana de Mendoza y la Cerda (1540–92), the only daughter of Diego de Mendoza, Prince of Mélito and grandson of the Great Cardenal Mendoza and Catalina de Silva. Told in the first person, the story begins much like *Urraca,* in which the protagonist, imprisoned behind guarded walls, discloses the political and the sexual adventures of her life and nearing death to her daughter Ana de Silva. But while this novel is reminiscent of *Urraca* and is marketed as both a historical novel and a love story, it does not apply the same stylistic techniques used to increase the erotic charge of Ortiz's narrative.

4. The exposure of sexually taboo topics parallels, for example, the use in Benetton ads of gay couples and interracial couples or children to wake their viewers up from the mass of images that surround them and to provoke a strong political response that will ensure the ads are noticed.

3

Voiceless Power: Fetishism in
Solitario de amor by Cristina Peri Rossi

Todos somo adictos a algo.
Entre dosis y dioses, sólo
hay una e de diferencia.
—Cristina Peri Rossi, *Inmovilidad de los barcos*

[We are all addicted to something. Between doses and gods there is
only an *e* of difference.]

It is not a new claim that advertising is a fetishistic medium or that it applies
the eroticized body to sell products, but in the eighties and nineties, advertising began to use the body as a substitute for products themselves. Ads that
include the nude body not only sell lotion, soap, gel, shampoo, and lingerie,
but they also promote credit cards, watches, jeans, and cars. Today, many ads
leave the realm of pure product recognition and use the human body to comment on the products' own construction. A Swatch watch ad that was published in several women's magazines (*Downtown* and *Cosmopolitan,* among
others) in Spain in 1998 exemplifies this phenomenon. The full-page, color ad
includes a female figure and a Swatch watch. The black (and in other versions
white) woman on the left side is surprised by the camera's seemingly fixed
stare. Her arms are crossed and her left leg is pulled toward her body in an
attempt to cover her nudity. Her fingers are extended in ecstasy and her body
retains the wetness of an afternoon swim. She wears nothing but a watch. The
"Skin" Swatch watch on the right side of the page is shown from both a frontal
and a side view and practically disappears into the white background of the
ad. The copy reads: "Estoy desnuda, ¿o no lo estoy?" (I am naked, or am I?).
The readers and viewers of this ad might answer, "yes and no," and wonder

whether the question concerns the body or the watch. While the watch fades into the whiteness of the paper, the contrast of the black female body on the white surface draws attention. The watch is naked, while the body is clothed with the visual power of viewers' erotic desires.

At the same time that the female figure attracts the sexual gaze of viewers, the image points to its own coming into being through the product that it is selling. The woman in the ad "is" because she is wearing a Swatch watch, and the watch "is" because its invisibility—its color and thinness—melts into the body that wears it. The watch becomes the second skin of the model and, as such, reflects a metonymic association. In Cristina Peri Rossi's *Solitario de amor* (Love Solitaire), as in the watch ad, the text re-presents the female body on different levels in order to fix it as the ever present second skin of the protagonist (or of the viewers). The connection that the novel establishes with the readers is expanded to include their imaginary and visual faculties in relation to the system that constructs the body in- and outside the text. In other words, the "Swatch watch woman" herself is a metonymic representation of the second skin that we, as viewers, would like either to be or to have.

Solitario exposes a process of fetishization through the limited perspective of an individual whose existence revolves around desire for his past lover. The novel highlights, as did the ad, the erotic dimension of the body and places it at the center of textual attention (as often occurs with the body of female authors). Because of the sexual and existential effects that the body has on the protagonist, the female figure becomes the site at which linguistic powers and limits can be discussed. The body enters a performative dimension in the sense that it intends to repeat and "normalize"—fix and make real—the narrator's experience. But the text disrupts its citational dimension through a performance that Peggy Phelan defines as "reproduction without repetition" (3), that is, an act in which the body cannot be frozen into one particular image. This process has already been hinted at in the chapter herein on Queen Urraca, who demonstrated that nobody could hold down the meaning attributed to her image—the sculpture that resided in the town's church as a sign of adultery. Depending on the context in which the female figure is placed and on each individual viewing position, signification takes on different forms. *Solitario* exemplifies this process even more clearly by adopting a male narrative voice that attempts to fetishize his female lover's body through visual and textual means. The text exposes the female body's ability to undermine fetishization and to reestablish itself from within the same system that constructs it, even though the female voice is absent throughout.

In the work of Peri Rossi, eroticism is a constant. Her collections of short stories, *Los museos abandonados* (The Abandoned Museums) and *Una pasión prohibida* (A Prohibited Passion), her novel *Solitario de amor,* and particularly *Fantasías eróticas* (Erotic Fantasies) establish her as one of the most important female writers in this traditionally male field. For Peri Rossi, eroticism is not disconnected from literature since the latter "es un acto de amor... un acto más complejo de amor" (is an act of love—a more complex act of love) (Pérez-Sánchez 64). Peri Rossi believes that, similar to the workings of fetishism, "la escritura [es] algo que [tiene] que ver con la magia" (writing is something that has to do with magic) (Riera 20). Less magical and more technical is the manner in which Peri Rossi uses erotic language to undermine established norms of literary and political sexual control. Elia Kantaris analyzes Peri Rossi's work in relation to the power and the alienation of male sexual politics construed around "the desire to possess, and in particular to monopolize the means of (re)production" (248). Peri Rossi, he says, uses "fragmentation, incoherence and disjunction as ways of escaping from the 'controlling structures' of repression" (263). Literature and language, he adds, are for Peri Rossi the arenas for battles of sexual identity.

In poetry as well as the novel, short story, and essay, Peri Rossi escapes the control of erotic identity on both a narrative and a thematic level. In her poetic work, especially in *Descripción de un naufragio* (Description of a Shipwreck), *Evohé,* and *Lingüística general* (General Linguistics), her dialectics of desire, as Hugo Verani calls it, moves through four different stages: direct erotic expression, irony and sarcasm, playful abundance, and the elevation of desire to mythical proportions. In other words, desire becomes the motor of mental liberation, and the body and the word become loci of rebellion (Verani 12). Graciela Mántaras Loedel calls Peri Rossi's erotic exposition in *Los museos abandonados* a "'momento cenital de la existencia. Toda la plenitud y la profundidad de lo vivo se asumen en ella y el eros es siempre un ritual, una liturgia, un ejercicio de misterio. Por eso, aunque gozoso y perfecto, no cabría llamarle alegre. En todo caso, su alegría es la que se conquista a través del dolor. Se recupera así una vivencia y una visión dramáticas del eros'" (a zenith moment of existence. All plenitude and depth of life are assumed in it and Eros is always a ritual, a liturgy, an exercise in mystery. For this reason, although joyful and perfect, it is not possible to call it happy. In any case, its happiness is one that one conquers through pain. In this manner one recuperates a dramatic experience and vision of Eros) (36). In *Una pasión prohibida,* the double edge of desire is further explored. This collection of short stories centers on the manner in which "'identity' is constructed or deconstructed at the borders and limits imposed upon desire" (Kantaris 250). In *Solitario,* this same desire crosses the borders of prohibition to expose itself as such: as pure desire for a female body. The novel establishes strong connections among the erotic, the aesthetic, and the linguistic. In her latest novel, *El amor es una droga dura* (Love Is a Hard Drug), Peri Rossi underlines the importance of the visual system of signification for erotic excitement.

Fantasías eróticas is perhaps Peri Rossi's most revealing display of erotic ideas. The book comprises a series of essays that range from a creative piece that takes place at a gay bar in Barcelona to essays that treat the construction of erotic fantasies through cross-dressing, prostitution, blow-up dolls, and the objectification of both males and females. In this tract on eroticism, Peri Rossi, says Rosemary Geisdorfer Feal, "breaks with traditional notions of that genre as one dominated by objectivity, rationality, and suppression of creative writing and of the fictional imagination. To write of erotica under the erasure of the erotic imagination is exactly what Peri Rossi has refused to do" (215). Peri Rossi comes full circle as she exposes the position that has exiled women from the erotic tradition while at the same time she opens the topic to the observers' views. Just as she does not separate the female erotic body from the person, she does not disassociate the language she uses from the topic she treats. *Fantasías eróticas* "both displaces eroticism from the stranglehold of masculinity . . . and recirculates it through the principal signs of power" (Geisdorfer Feal 216). Peri Rossi writes about what many women have not dared to express because "es evidente que las mujeres no han querido decirles a los hombres la verdad. La verdad la dicen las mujeres en la peluquería" (it is evident that women have not wanted to tell men the truth. Women only tell the truth in the hair salon) (Riera 24). One might say that Peri Rossi is one of the major female spokespeople for all that eroticism has kept secret.

Solitario, as one critic put it, is a story without a story. Mántaras Loedel refers to a story that revolves around one axis: the infatuation of an anonymous male narrator with a woman who has left him. According to Peri Rossi, the novel was written in six months, and only three words were changed in its published version (Riera 20). The dominant character-focalizer paraphrases his ex-lover Aída's thoughts and interrupts himself intermittently with the discourse of his interlocutor, Raúl.[1] The internal focalization not only is limiting but the protagonist—"no tiene nombre. No tiene cara, estatura, color de pelo, nacionalidad, padres, pasado. Su ser no es otro que ser-amante" (has no name. He has no face, size, hair color, nationality, parents, past. His being is no other than a lover-being) (Mántaras Loedel 39)—points to the overall theme of the erotic in this novel as a closed and individual realm that does not allow the protagonist to conceive of a separate existence.[2] The novel reflects the intensity of passion in two ways: the manner in which the anonymous character perceives his love and infatuation with Aída and the way the narrative closes off other points of view to the readers. The narrative act and technique mirror their thematic counterpart.

The protagonist remembers in order to recapture the love and passion that he has lost. He rearticulates and relives his intimate experiences with Aída and thereby comes to realize the inability of words to return him to his past state of amorous fulfillment. Linda Hutcheon would call this a work of linguistic metafiction in which self-reflection leads to a realization of the powers and the limits of language (23). Peri Rossi's novel is more than self-critical, however, for language is eroticized through explicitly sexual encounters and increasing metaphorical references to Aída's body. When narrative is eroticized, the body, not the text, becomes the site at which metafictional dimensions can be discussed. The movement is similar to that in advertising when the eroticized body and the fading recognition of the product ask readers or viewers to think about the construction of the ad. Both advertising and narrative, in this case, are based on fetishism, whereby they place the body at the center of visual and textual attention.

Some say that "'we are all more or less fetishists'" (qtd. in Steele 11).[3] Because the term *fetishism* is packed with negative connotations, not many people would approve of being called a fetishist even if the smile, nose, foot, or shoelace of a lover is what one most desires when the lover is absent. But Marta, a single teacher and the protagonist of Peri Rossi's "Fetichistas S.A." in *Desastres íntimos* (Intimate Disasters), actually admits to being a person who "no [está] bien de cabeza" (is not sane) (18). Her experience serves as a useful register for the definition of fetishism. Marta's fetishism consists of the following: "a veces [dice ella], me enloquezco por un cuello largo, estilizado, con forma de pino, esos cuellos que ascienden hasta las alturas y hacen pensar que quien lo porta es un soñador, una criatura romántica; otras veces, en cambio, me siento irresistiblemente atraída por un cuello con una nuez de Adán prominente, que sobresale, como un pene en erección" (sometimes [she says] I go crazy for a long neck, stylized, in the form of a pine, like those necks that rise to the heights and make one believe that he who carries it is a dreamer, a romantic creature; other times, on the other hand, I feel irresistibly attracted to necks with a prominent Adam's apple that bulges out like an erect penis) (12). Her lover Fernando has one of the most fascinating Adam's apples that she has seen. She insists that her love for his neck does not invalidate her love for him as a person: "No era menos amor porque estuviera tan específicamente dirigido a su cuello. ¿Por qué iba a amarlo más, si repartiera ese amor entre sus otras partes?" (It was no less love because it was specifically directed to his neck. Why would I love him more if I were to divide this love among his other parts?) (19–20). Marta points to a fundamental aspect of fetishism, which is the substitution of a part for the whole and the confusion "of the power an object represents with the object itself, the taking of a sign for the thing" (Steiner 82); in Marta's case, she takes the Adam's apple as a sign for the penis.

The conversion of the other—which can take on an infinite number of forms—into a significant fetishized object lies in the individual's power of subjective vision "porque es la *mirada* quien les presta valor" (because it is the look that lends it value) (Peri Rossi, *Desastres* 17). Fetishization depends on the perspective of the onlooker. It is deeply rooted, as Wendy Steiner explains, in the history of the term, which derives from the Portuguese word *feitiço* and was applied first by fifteenth-century Portuguese traders to describe the cult objects of West Africa used in witchcraft. The word then entered other European languages in the eighteenth century with the new study of comparative religion, when a fetish was a statue or other object thought by a "primitive" culture to be the dwelling place of a powerful spirit. In these usages, *fetish* involves a discrepancy between those who believe in the fetish object and those who look at it from the outside, who judge the fetishist deluded, primitive, or pagan. The fetishist's error supposedly lies in the habit of fetishizing per se, but, in fact, it consists in choosing the "wrong" fetishes. Those same Portuguese traders, after all, protected themselves from harm by wearing medals of Catholic saints and bowing down before holy relics (Steiner 81).

Whether the fetishized object is a voodoo doll, an image of a Catholic deity, or a lover's neck, the term *fetishism* has served to support the authority of the outsider. What Marta may find fascinatingly stimulating and meaningful may be abominably banal, foreign, and sick to Fernando: "Porque la relación que uno establece con su fetiche (sean las medias de naylon negras, las campanas de una máquina llena de luces o un vaso de whisky) es siempre personal, intransferible, solitaria e intensa" (Because the relationship that one establishes with one's fetish [be it black nylon stockings, bells in a machine full of lights, or a glass of whisky] is always personal, intransferable, solitary, and intense) (11), says Marta. For her, necks have much to do with this century-long magical tradition of fetishization. The meaning that is attributed to the object is similar to "lo maravilloso [que] nunca está en la superficie, hay que sumergirse para hallarlo; lo maravilloso es periférico, marginal, oculto, un túnel, un mundo hundido, una zona del limbo" (the wonderful that is never on the surface, one must submerge in order to find it; the beautiful is peripheral, marginal, hidden, a tunnel, a sunken world, a zone in limbo) (87). Fetishism is an interior, semireligious moment that belongs to a world so on the edge that its subjects will do most anything to achieve the experience and hide its effects.

Fetishization is an act of seduction: the object seduces the viewer as much as the viewer seduces the object. As Marta says, "siento que todos esos cuellos me están mirando" (I feel like all those necks are looking at me) (24). Yet, for Marta, the object is not only given life and a vision with which to seduce her, but it is endowed with a new identity. For some, this identity is all-fulfilling; for others, such as Fernando, it provokes an uncanny feeling of being watched: "Qué curioso, [dice Marta]. Yo sé que soy fetichista, pero hasta entonces no me había dado cuenta de que él era un poco paranoico. Los cuellos no son ojos, Fernando: son sexos" (how curious [says Marta]. I know that I am a fetishist, but until then I had not realized that he was a bit paranoid. Necks are not eyes, Fernando: they are genitalia) (24).[4] The ironic twist of these last lines in Peri Rossi's story renders fetishism multifold by pointing to its subjective dimensions of transformation, uncanniness, and seduction: necks = eyes = sex.

If eroticism affects—rejects, enhances, changes—the sexual or sensual response of a subject through aesthetic elements, fetishism overemphasizes aesthetic vision by focusing on one particular element and making it real. Marta explains this process in her definition of fetishism: "Según los tratados de psicología, los fetichistas toman la parte por el todo: un pie, los ojos, los senos, una prenda o un objeto representan el todo, y hacia esa parte o ese objeto experimentan una suerte de mística adoración, como el fiel ante la divinidad. Leímos esa definición en el club y consideramos que estaba parcialmente equivocada: para nosotros, una parte . . . no *representa* el todo, sino que *es* el todo" (According to psychological treatise, fetishists take the part for the whole: a foot, the eyes, the breast, a garment, or an object represent the whole, and toward that part or object they experience a fortune of mystic adoration, like a believer in front of a deity. We read this definition in the club and we felt that it was partially incorrect: for us, a part . . . does not *represent* the whole but it *is* the whole) (19). Aestheticization breaks down the barrier between the object and the subject, the same and the other, and the viewer identifies totally with the fetishized element (same = other). The process is one of erotic self-fulfillment that ignores divisions and obstacles as the subject continuously tries to satisfy his or her own imaginary infatuation with the desired element.

For Marta, then, fetishism is a process of loss, of desire, and of sublimation.[5] William Pietz reflects on another aspect of fetishism: "The fetish is always a meaningful fixation of a singular event; it is above all a 'historical' object, the enduring material form and force of an unrepeatable event" (Apter and Pietz 3).[6] What interests me here is how fetishism is related to fixation. On a psychoanalytical level, fixation "refers to the fact that the libido attaches itself firmly to persons or imagos, that it reproduces a particular mode of satisfaction, [and] that it retains an organization that is in accordance with the characteristic structure of one of its stages of development" (Laplanche and Pontalis 162). While fetishism refers to the product and the ultimate goal for which *Solitario* is written—to have a representation of Aída stand in for Aída herself—fixation comments on the process and the medium used to fetishize.

The psychoanalytical tone that underlies fetishism is strongly present throughout *Solitario.* Love and desire are already set in a negative relation to each other through the two epigraphs that launch the novel. The first is an excerpt from a poem by Paul Valéry: "los gestos extraños / que para matar el Amor / hacen los amantes" (the strange gestures / that to kill Love / lovers make). The second reflects on the underlying Lacanian discourse of the novel: "Amar es dar lo que no se tiene a quien no es" (To love is to give what one does not have to one who is not). Instead of placing love within its all-encompassing myth of fulfillment, these epigraphs look at love in a negative and destructive light. Consequently, the novel puts not only the female object of desire, Aída, in the position of the unattainable (m)other, but it also connects the desire for the body to writing because the imaginary "behaves in precisely the same way as language: it moves ceaselessly on from object to object or from signifier to signifier, and will never find full and present satisfaction just as meaning can never be seized as full presence" (Moi 101). While such a psychoanalytical interpretation is pertinent, these two epigraphs lend themselves to a consumerist reading. The epigraphs from Valéry and Lacan comment on a product—desire, love—that needs to be disrupted and rejected before and after it is possessed. The product is disembodied in the sense that it resides within yet without the body: the body stands in for the product. The object or the subject—"Amar es dar lo que no se tiene"—in theory, buys the product for or gives it to a person—"a quien no es"— who identifies with the body in the ad. The ad, as the novel, refers to a love that does not physically exist. Existence and nonexistence play tug-of-war between gestures that point to corporeal power and corporeal absence. The body and the idea, movement and stasis, are interrelated and transformed into an aberration of continuous desire.

At the end of *Solitario,* the narrator materializes the process of impossible physical embodiment through the act of writing. In a train on his way to his mother's house, the protagonist flees from his feelings for Aída, who has ended their relationship. He compares the acceleration of the train to an erotic interlude, or climax, of Aída's. Aída's orgasm comes about at the same time that the train's speed increases and at the moment that a second voice, in italics, interjects itself into the imaginary consciousness of the narrator's writing process and recites the Hebrew saying, "Cuando la pasión te ciegue, / vístete de negro / y vete adonde nadie te conozca" (When passion blinds you / dress in black / and go there where nobody knows you) (183). This same voice, projected on the flowers, horses, and lilies in the field, also repeats three times *"te conocemos"* (we know you) (185). Are the readers perhaps the subjects of this verb? Are they looking from the outside in? For the first time in the narrative, there is a heightened awareness of the power that love plays in the protagonist's text. Love blinds. The narrator cannot see the landscape that is rapidly passing outside his train window. He therefore goes where nobody knows him and where biological vision is unnecessary: he escapes into the text and into the arms of the readers. He attempts to reli(e)ve his erotic relationship with Aída. The process may be a painful one, but "el dolor es mi última manera de estar con Aída, de serle fiel, de prolongar mi pasión" (pain is my last means to be with Aída, to be loyal to her, to prolong my passion) (179). In addition to writing, Aída becomes a medium that allows his being to enter into existence, for "si ella no me nombra, soy un ser anónimo" (if she does not name me, I am an anonymous being) (179). The more erotic the narration, the closer the pen/penis comes to fulfilling his disembodied love. The last paragraphs of the novel suggest that the actual text that the readers hold in their hands may be the same one that the protagonist begins to write in the train as he slowly loses sight of the landscape and loses himself on the page in erotic memories of passion.

Writing is not only related to passion and eroticism, but it is specifically linked to the body. To understand fully this connection, it is worth looking at the trajectory that the protagonist attributes to language: it erupts out of "una oculta caverna, . . . surge, revienta del fondo olvidado de mi infancia, estalla con su fuerza primigenia" (a hidden cave, . . . it appears, it bursts out of the forgotten depth of my infancy, it explodes with its original strength) (15, 17). Once language leaves the darkness of the past, it is associated with the touch of the narrator before it takes on meaning: "La palpo como quien ha de (re)conocer antes de nombrar" (I touch her like someone who must recognize [and know] before naming) (17). As the narrator recognizes Aída's body and turns her moans into pleasurable cries, language—now literally in his hands—is portrayed as a medium stripped of all ideological baggage: "[Aída es] un desnudo limpio, sin residuos nocturnos, sin adherencias. Como si siempre estuviera recién salida del baño. Entonces las palabras, las viejas palabras de toda la vida, aparecen, súbitamente, ellas también desnudas, frescas, resplandecientes, crudas, con toda su potencia, con todo su peso, desprendidas del uso, en toda su pureza, como si se hubiera bañado en una fuente primigenia"

([Aída is] a clean nude without nocturnal residues, without adherences. As if she were always stepping out of the bathtub. Then the words, the old eternal words, appear, suddenly, also undressed, fresh, shining, crude, with all their power, with all their weight, detached from use, in all their purity, as if they had been bathed in an original fountain) (14–15).

Aída's body functions like a pure sheet of paper stroked by a fountain pen's pristine ink. As the protagonist heightens Aída's sexual responses through his caressing words, he also establishes his own existence and his power at creation: "nazco entre las sábanas de Aída y conmigo nacen otras palabras, otros sonidos, muerte y resurrección" (I am born between Aída's sheets and with me other words and sounds, death and resurrection, are born) (15). The eroticization of narrative points to the female body and to its sexual performance as that which allows language to evolve and create new meanings. Writing takes on a performative dimension through eroticization.

Not all descriptions of Aída's body are erotic. On the contrary, there are moments when conventional language is used to express scientific definitions of her organs: "El lenguaje convencional estalla. . . . Cobro una lucidez repentina acerca del lenguaje. . . . Nazco y me despojo de eufemismos; no amo su cuerpo, estoy amando su hígado membranoso de imperceptible pálpito, la blanca esclerótica de sus ojos, el endometrio sangrante, el lóbulo agujereado" (Conventional language explodes. . . . I attain a sudden lucidity concerning language. . . . I am born and I strip myself of euphemisms; I do not love her body, I am loving her membraned kidney of unperceivable palpitations, the white sclera of her eyes, the bloody endometrium, the pierced earlobe) (15–16). The protagonist's anatomical language goes beyond the skin in an exaggerated attempt to penetrate the other's body. Lucidity is related to a feeling of love that is expressed beyond metaphors and euphemisms and ever more emphatically connects passion to language and the body. The discourse of love, in its scientific or poetic form, is the only possible manner of communication for the protagonist. He and Aída, he proclaims, "*Nos amamos en lenguas*" (Love each other in languages/tongues) (22); while the word *lengua* here may imply his tongue on his lover's skin or his tongue as it searches for her most inner and minute particles, it also refers to language as the primary tool of amorous communication, since *lengua* in Spanish may be translated as both *language* and *tongue*.

The continuous desire to capture the body in writing reflects language's own power and limitations. In advertising, this dimension, as I have already mentioned, has come about through the increase in erotic images of both female and male bodies and the decrease in product recognition and association. In *Solitario,* the metafictional process is linked to Aída and to the nam-

ing and touching of her body: "Voy poniendo nombres a las partes de Aída, soy el primer hombre, asombrado y azorado, balbuceante, babeante, babélico, y en medio de la confusión de mi nacimiento, inmerso en el misterio, murmuro sonidos viscerales que (re)conocer. Palpo su cuerpo, imagen del mundo, y bautizo los órganos; emocionado, saco palabras como piedras arcaicas y las instalo en las partes de Aída, como eslabones de mi ignorancia" (I am starting to name the body parts of Aída; I am the first man, surprised and startled, stammering, drooling, unintelligible, and in the midst of the confusion of my birth, immersed in the mystery; I murmur visceral sounds to be recognized/known. I touch her body, image of the world, and I baptize the organs; moved, I extract words like archaic stones and I install them on Aída's parts, like links of my ignorance) (18). Aída's body stirs up emotions and evokes words that are born out of prehistory. The past and the present as well as time and space are conflated. The protagonist has a dual function in this novel: he is the author of the text the public is reading and the author of the body he sculpts. The word and the image come together in a simultaneous process of creation and delineation.

The protagonist of *Solitario* lives, he says, in an infinite time, a time without past, a time of waiting, a time of obsession, an imaginary time in which he is "separado del resto del mundo, adherido umbilicalmente al tiempo sólo por un estrecho cordón llamado Aída" (separated from the rest of the world, tied umbilically to time only by a thin string called Aída) (73). To the question "¿Pasa el tiempo?" (Does time pass?) the narrator gives the answer: "Instalado en una eternidad fija como un lago de cristal me vuelvo inmutable, perenne: tengo una sola dimensión, la del espacio. Los poros te miran, te miran las venas, las arterias y las cavidades" (Installed in a static eternity, like a crystal lake, I become immutable, perennial: I only have one dimension, that of space. The pores look at you, the veins look at you, the arteries and the cavities) (12). His look turns into a "contemplación estática" (fixed contemplation). Just as the protagonist might stand in front of the nude Aída, the readers can imagine themselves standing—immobile—in front of a billboard whose image has captured their libidinal attention to the fullest. They are in a position of fixed contemplation where nothing around them exists but this nude figure before them and their own look that forms and transforms their identities in the following manner:

> Mi mirada (mi múltiple mirada: te miro desde el pasado remoto del mar y de la piedra, del hombre y de la mujer neolíticos, del antiguo pez que fuimos una vez lejana, del volcán que nos arrojó, de la madera tallada, de la pesca y de la caza; te miro desde otros que no son enteramente yo y sin embargo; te miro desde la fría lucidez de tu madre y la confusa pasión de tu padre, desde el rencor de tu hermano y la envidia menoscabante de mis amigas; te miro desde mi avergon-

zado macho cabrío y desde mi parte de mujer enamorada de otra mujer; te miro desde la vejez que a veces—"Estoy cansada", dices—asoma en tus orejas, en las arrugas de la frente), hipnotizada, la sigue, perruna, hambrienta, pasiva y paciente. (11–12)

[My look (my multiple look: I look at you from the remote past of the sea and of the stone, from the neolithic man and woman, from the ancient fish that we were a long time ago, from the volcano that erupted us, from the carved wood, from fishing and hunting; I look at you from others who are not entirely me nonetheless; I look at you from the cold lucidity of your mother and the confused passion of your father, from the resentment of your brother and the damaging envy of your girlfriends; I look at you from my ashamed lustful manhood and from my part woman in love with another woman; I look at you from the old age that at times—"I am tired," you say—appears in your ears, in the wrinkles around your forehead), hypnotized, he follows her, doglike, hungry, passive, and patient.]

The parenthesis that almost entirely makes up this quotation extends the simplicity of a particular, passive, and patient look to one that transcends time, space, form, and gender. The public nature of the nude image in an advertisement, even though directed toward a well-researched target market, presents itself to a similar range of possible spectators and sexual orientations. Because of the importance given to transgressions in *Solitario,* what seems like another narrative of a heterosexual man fetishizing a female body opens itself up to an erotic display of infinite readers and characters. Peri Rossi's well-known adoption of the masculine voice in her work does not only undermine gender assumptions, but it takes on a variety of forms, among them a woman in love with another woman.[7]

The protagonist exposes his narrative through a continuous interior monologue that does not allow readers to pinpoint any specific time or place or identity. The anonymity and textual openness reflect the purpose of the narrative: to capture what is absent, the object of desire; or, as Brooks puts it: "narrative is thus generated as both approach and avoidance, the story of desire that can never quite speak its name nor quite attain its object" (103). This is the same device that propels the success of advertising; both are based on desire. And both *Solitario* and advertising place the object at the center of narration and focus on the body as their narrative plot. In each case, the readers and viewers do not have a stable, fixed image on which to rest their eyes. Instead, "*De mirar* hemos pasado *a ver mirar* y donde antes la mirada se llenaba con la presencia de un objeto que tendía a colmarla, ahora encontramos un espacio para el despliegue de acercamientos y distancias, de identificaciones y rupturas, de tentaciones y provocaciones, de intimidaciones y seducciones"

(*From seeing,* we have passed to *seeing one look,* and where before the look was filled with the presence of an object that tended to fulfill it, now we find a space for the deployment of approaches and distances, of identifications and ruptures, of temptations and provocations, of intimidations and seductions) (Zunzunegui 14). The images are in constant flux; they seduce and tease the readers' imagination. The interior monologue and textual openness of *Solitario* advance the idea that "el universo de los anuncios no es tanto 'crear necesidades' cuanto realimentar esa carencia profunda que nunca podrá ser colmada" (the universe of advertisements does not so much 'create needs' but renourish that deep lack that is never fulfilled) (Zunzunegui 15). In essence, writing is just that: the need to put into being that which does not exist. Both advertising and narrative are therefore fetishistic and metonymic processes: "It is as if the frustrated attempt to fix the body in the field of vision set off the restless movement of narrative, telling the story of approach to, and swerve away from, that final object of sight that cannot be contemplated" (Brooks 103). Since the narrator cannot hold onto Aída's body in the field of vision, he fetishizes vision itself. When he looks at Aída's breasts, he thinks of them as a second pair of eyes: "Siento que me miras con dos pares de ojos: los de tu cara que se pasean por mi cuerpo desnudo y los ojos de tus senos, que buscan el rostro, que examinan mi boca, mi nariz, la frente, las mejillas" (I feel that you are looking at me with two pair of eyes: those of your face that travel along my naked body, and the eyes of your breasts that search my face, that examine my mouth, my nose, my forehead, my cheeks) (21). Her blouse becomes a balcony and her breasts, "curiosos, como mujeres, se asoman para mirar hacia afuera, no soportan mucho tiempo la vida de clausura" (curious, like women, lean to look outside, they do not bear for a long time the cloistered life) (21). Her breasts are personified as the eyes of a woman who, when covered with clothes, feels imprisoned and blinded. When this happens, "sólo te quedan los ojos de la cara para mirarme, y yo siento nostalgia por los otros" (only the eyes of your face are left to look at me, and I feel nostalgia for the others) (21). The conflation of Aída's breasts with her eyes takes place when the protagonist compares her with a painting by René Magritte: "Provista sólo con los ojos de la cara, Aída es una mujer indiferente: le falta algo, como a las mujeres de los cuadros de Magritte" (Provided with only the eyes of the face, Aída is an indifferent woman: she lacks something, like the women of the paintings by Magritte) (21). A painting that comes to mind in this scene is Magritte's *Le Viol* (fig. 6). The image displays a female face that is replaced by female body parts: breasts represent the eyes, a navel the nose, and pubic hair stands in for the woman's mouth. In this painting, the female body returns the gaze of which she is the object and renders that gaze (the

Figure 6. René Magritte, *Le Viol*, 1934. (© 2002 C. Herscovici, Brussels/Artists Rights Society [ARS], New York)

sexualized gaze) absurd. The painting disturbs the viewers' imagination because the nude body stands in for the face, and the eyes of the female figure look at the viewers provokingly as if to say: "Isn't this what you really want to see?" The body, when denied a head, becomes a costume for the look that interpellates the desire of the viewers. Vision is in constant flux and in constant metamorphosis; it displays the different manifestations of desire.

Vision is not about trying to see Aída more clearly but about increasing desire. It might seem as if blindness takes away from corporality, but the substitution of touch for sight—"No la toco: la palpo con la impudicia de un ciego" (I do not touch her: I feel her with the immodesty of a blind man) (6)—gives the body a material form and an erotic dimension that includes an entire series of sensations not accessible to the eye. This is where the path splits: it moves from eroticism to sexuality—sexuality being the tactile consequence of erotic desire—and from eroticism to idealization—idealization belonging to the sphere where clear, objective vision is obscured by desire (sometimes also called "love").

The protagonist then closes his eyes and displaces the touched to memory: "Los ciegos no ven: reconocen. Los ojos sin luz de los ciegos no se dirigen a las cosas o a los seres—que no ven—, sino a unos modelos ideales, abstractos. . . . Los ojos de los ciegos no están a la altura de los objetos terrenales, sino más arriba: en el espacio del sueño" (Blind people do not see: they recognize. The lightless eyes of the blind men do not direct themselves to things or to beings—that do not see—but to ideal, abstract models. The eyes of blind people are not at the same latitude as earthly objects, but higher: in the space of the dreams) (16). The touch then questions the validity of familiarization and of recognition: "el mensaje de las manos . . . es remitido a la memoria de la especie, a unos modelos ideales de los cuales el objeto es sólo una de las posibles representaciones" (the message of the hands . . . is sent to the memory of the species, to a series of ideal models of which the object is only one of all possible representations) (16)—as is the object of desire (be it the product or the body) in an advertisement. Blindness allows the narrator to reside in difference and multiplicity. Aída can be transformed into one of many materializations of an erotic species.

The narrative technique of the novel reflects the connection between blindness and memory. Written in the first-person present tense that refers to a past moment, or the historical present, the novel plays with the ambiguity and confusion of the past and the present, of Aída and her idealized image. The narrator does this by dividing his vision into two simultaneous looks: "la aparente que recorre la superficie, y la mirada del ciego, que remite lo mirado a la memoria de la especie" (the apparent one that travels over the surface, and the look of the blind person who remits the seen to the memory of the species) (17). When he touches Aída's breast, "la tierra y su imagen se acercan progresivamente" (earth and its image progressively approach one another) (17). He collapses the two realms that make up the text as the site for his memory. Past and present are joined in matrimonial harmony—or so the readers think. Until Aída declares through the narrator's voice that she does not want to reside in anybody's mind: "No quise ser el sueño de mi primer amante. . . . No quise ser, tampoco, el sueño [del segundo]" (I did not want to be the dream of my first lover . . . nor did I want to be the dream [of the second]) (148). The narrator realizes that Aída will love him only if he has no dream at all. If this is the case, the image that he remits to memory, and therefore to words, must not exist. He must annihilate the text itself, his entire fiction and the desire to capture her through language. What, then, would happen to *Solitario*?

Love does not take place through the annihilation of the text. The text exists because of the absence of the loved one. The question, then, is, "How does the protagonist reclaim his passion if not by capturing her body through an idealized image?" This is where the text comes full circle back to its epigraphs. The object of desire is always once removed because it mentally and visually resides in the shop window, on the billboard, or in the magazine ad. The protagonist can come closest to this object by being consumed by it; he must reduce himself to a product of desire.

An ad for Cerámica Zirconio tiles (fig. 7), published in 1988, the same year as *Solitario,* shows how the narrator might be able to approach Aída. The copy reads:

> Bella y suave. Cálida y resistente.
>   Sobria y elegante.
> Es cerámica Zirconio. Un revestimiento tan íntimo,
>   adaptable y perfecto como una segunda piel.
> La piel de tu casa.
> Zirconio. Piel de cerámica.
>
> [Beautiful and smooth, hot and resistant.
>   Moderate and elegant.
> It is Zirconio ceramics. A lining so intimate,
>   adaptable and perfect like a second skin.
> The skin of your house.
> Zirconio. Ceramic skin.]

The poetic form of the advertising message allows for a certain degree of metaphoric and metonymic liberties. Poetry becomes the "creative imitation of the sensual" (Kahmen 10). The first two lines are not exactly a masterpiece of

Figure 7.   Advertisement for Cerámica Zirconio tiles created by Delvico Bates Advertising in 1988. (Reprinted with the permission of Export-Zirconio, Zirconio S.A.)

erotic sensuality, but they do create a certain seductive image of a woman whose soft skin evokes both desire and elegant resistance. In effect, the contours of the torso are very appealing to the eye and create a harmonious composition through the black and white shading and the vertical lines of the stretched-out arms and legs. This figure could be the body of the protagonist's lover in *Solitario*. She is the person whom the narrator is writing about. The writer of *Solitario* is of one identity; "Su ser no es otro que ser-amante" (His being is no other than that of a lover-being) (Mántaras Loedel 39). To insist that the copywriter of the Delvico Bates agency who produced this ad is no other than an anonymous lover-being would probably not be acceptable— even though he or she might agree—but one could claim that the ad may be read as a "ser-amante," a product whose image may be conceived of as a lover-substitute as it tries to fulfill the viewers' imaginary desires through a visual representation.

So, as the readers or viewers sit in a hot, steamy tub filled with scented bathwater, they may look up and see the image of the sexy body in the ad reflected on the Zirconio ceramic tiles of their new and improved home. In this intimate setting, the image may be truly adaptable, as the ad says, to the architecture of consumers' walls or to the preferences of their imaginations. In any case, there it is before them, the performance of an ad whose message promised them desire and fulfillment. They believe they see, through the thickening steam, the female body portrayed on their Cerámica Zirconio tiles. To their dismay, the figure in this ad is not a perceptible and palpable second skin, as the ad suggests, but the second skin of their cold bathroom walls, and the second skin of a tree trunk, in other words, the paper of the magazines and billboard ads where this image will forever rest.

Once the image pulls the viewers into the ad or the narrative through its erotic elements, both men and women, homosexual or heterosexual, are themselves in danger of becoming publicized. They are made aware of the distance between the body viewed, the body desired, and the body that exists in real life (as is the narrator). For the protagonist of *Solitario* to close in on the body he sees, he needs to buy a second skin. This is the only way that he can actually approach Aída. Buying a second skin allows him, he believes, to break down the barrier of distance. One day, while walking down the street, he sees "un anuncio en una vitrina [que] muestra a una modelo cubierta por una malla negra, de nailon, y me asombro de que no sea Aída. Entro en la tienda, en seguida, y compro la malla" (an advertisement in a shop window that displays a model covered by a black, nylon leotard, and I am surprised that it is not Aída. I go into the store at once and buy the leotard) (123). Therein, the text exposes a scene of a sexual encounter in which Aída tells him: "Cúbreme . . . honda, solemne" (Cover me . . . deep, solemn) (125). He covers her with his body just like "la malla negra [que] me representa, me simboliza, ejecuta por mí lo que yo no puedo hacer: no puedo, aunque quiero, ser nada más que un tejido de nailon bordado, delgado como un hilo, pegado a su piel. Pero no es otro mi deseo: quisiera ser la malla, quisiera ser la tela sobre su cuerpo, no tener más vida ni más consistencia que ésa. Si fuera la malla negra, podría estar todo el tiempo sobre su piel, ciñéndola, de los pies al escote" (the leotard that represents me, symbolizes me, executes for me what I cannot do: I cannot, even though I want to, be anything more than a piece of embroidered material, thin like a thread, glued to her skin. But none other is my desire: I would like to be the leotard, I would like to be the fabric on her body, not to have more life or consistency than that. If I were that black leotard, I could be on her skin all the time, encircling her from the feet to the neck) (124). His sexual act and body stand in for the clothing piece that he can never be. He knows that the only way for him to seduce the body on paper, the same body that he is writing about and the same body that he is creating and seducing through vision, is by being the body in the ad. Advertising, says Zunzunegui, "se descubre como un guante que se ajusta a la perfección a la piel de una sociedad que, de represora del cuerpo y sus pulsiones, ha pasado a glorificadora de la dimensión sensible de la experiencia" (is discovered like a glove that fits to perfection to the skin of a society that, initially repressive of the body and its pulsations, has passed to glorifying the sensitive dimension of the experience) (6). Similar to this definition of advertising, the protagonist desires to fit himself to the female body like a glove. To his dismay, his lover pushes him away and resists being covered by this male skin "como si la ropa [para Aída] fuera una segunda piel, incómoda, un disfraz levemente opuesto. El vestido es la interdicción" (as if clothing [for Aída] were a second skin, uncomfortable, a slightly opposed diguise. The piece of clothing is prohibition) (22). Aída rejects being clothed; she rejects that her visually exposed body be covered by the product it promotes. Her nudity in this case represents her liberation.

When one pushes the analogy between the Cerámica Zirconio ad and *Solitario* a little bit further, the protagonist becomes the key that opens the door to the house. At the beginning of the novel, the narrator wishes to construct Aída a home in which to live, a home that is "acogedora como el vientre de una madre" (welcoming like the womb of a mother) (25). Like the second skin, Aída rejects this proposition and undermines the viewer by becoming what he wants to place her in. If he cannot place her in a house, he will turn her into one: "El sexo de Aída es una cerradura. Intervengo en él como el extranjero dotado de una llave que abre la puerta para explorar la casa extraña" (Aída's sex is a lock that opens the door to explore the strange house) (35). By turning her into a home, he can have access to her since she is the lock and he is the key that opens the lock. But just as she rejected him as her "segunda piel" (second skin), she also rejects him as "la piel de tu casa" (the skin of your home) because both are the same on a metonymical level and both serve to fetishize her.

At the end of the novel, Aída literally denies him access to her home: "Aída me había echado de su casa, de su útero, de su habitación, de su cuerpo" (Aída has thrown me out of her house, her uterus, her room, her body) (169). In the ad for Cerámica Zirconio, the product is reduced to a second skin, and the second skin is equated to the skin of one's bathroom walls and one's home. In *Solitario,* the narrator wishes to be the product that covers the body exposed in the ad—the second skin. Only this time, the tile is a piece of clothing and the body is Aída's. The visually and textually eroticized body animates, disrupts, and seduces an always absent other.

When Aída throws the protagonist out of her house and her life, she cries out: "¡Por fin te he parido!" (Finally, I have given birth to you!). With this cry she frees herself from the subject who has been trying to reproduce her through various means. The rupture that these last words represent is the one that cuts the umbilical cord of fetishism. Similar to the way the body resists being fixed through a mechanical reproduction, she frees herself from the sexual reproduction of her biological sex. Even though Aída has no voice in this novel, the fact that the text evolves because of her decision to end her relationship with the protagonist makes her agency present. Even though her body is the principal site of fetishization, it continuously resists being fixated upon. The text reflects what Peggy Phelan describes in relation to performativity as a "reproduction without repetition" (3), whereby Aída's being only resides in the presence of her own nudity. Her figure can never be reproduced or pinned down into one determinate signification or source of desire. *Solitario* allows one "to invent a politically implicated language of cultural interpretation that somehow desublimates the inherent voyeurism of the critic's fixative stare" (Apter and Pietz 9). Peri Rossi's novel points to the erotic performance of the female body as a site of resistance, a site that may be attributed to woman inside and outside of the text. What this resistance permits is a discourse that opens up new possibilities for female writers in Spain: it allows for language to defy logical narrative by associating itself with passion, love, and sexuality. It transgresses time, space, and gender and propels an infinite display of spectators and writers. It rewrites the private into the public sphere and gives new importance to the visual field as an inherent part of the system that creates and interprets the liberated nude body. It shows how erotic language can create and resist, at the same time and within the same process, an act that tries to delimit the contours of woman.

Notes

1. The "character-focalizer" is not to be confused with a "narrator-focalizer," who, according to Rimmon-Kenan, is linked to an external focalization (74).

2. Peri Rossi responds to the statement "Lo que domina *Solitario de amor* es la pasión" (What dominates *Solitario de amor* is passion) with "Exactamente. Es un mundo cerrado" (Exactly. It is a closed world) (Riera 23).

3. Freud, in *Three Essays on the Theory of Sexuality,* says: "A certain degree of fetishism is . . . habitually present in normal love, especially in those stages of it in which the normal sexual aim seems unattainable or its fulfillment prevented" (20).

4. Marta turns necks into genitalia. This is a specifically Freudian process of fetishization that "makes a part of another's body into a phallus" (Wright 117).

5. Freud considers fetishism as linked to the libido and the female body. He describes the term in *Three Essays on the Theory of Sexuality:* "What is substituted for the sexual object is some part of the body (such as the foot or the hair) which is in general very inappropriate for sexual purposes, or some inanimate object which bears an assignable relation to the person whom it replaces and preferably to that person's sex-

uality" (19). What interests Freud is the pathological aspect of fetishism, the moment when the object takes the place of the loved person and "becomes the *sole* sexual object" (20). He points to the connection of fetishism to a thought, symbol, or repression from childhood. In "Minutes from the Vienna Psychoanalytic Society," he further develops this relation to a lost instinctual pleasure experienced in childhood or in reminiscences of beloved persons. While part of the experience from infancy is suppressed, the other half is metonymically fetishized into an object. The process includes a "suppression of instinct, partial repression, and elevation of a portion of the repressed complex to an ideal" (158). In his 1927 essay "Fetishism," he relates the concept to an exclusively male behavior, in which the fetish is substituted for the mother's missing penis. Freud makes fetishism a purely male perversion—a major point of feminist criticism and the major reason why I do not undertake an outright Freudian analysis of *Solitario*.

6. For more information on the theory of fetishism, see Gamman and Makinen, Apter, Mulvey, and Stratton, among others.

7. Helena Antolín Cochrane says that Peri Rossi, "As a woman author, and a lesbian . . . not only uses language thematically to question depictions of the feminine but frequently also deliberately adopts a masculine voice in order to undermine automatic gender assumptions and to challenge her readers who might suppose that one can linguistically detect the difference between masculine and feminine" (98). Antolín Cochrane also states that Peri Rossi uses the masculine voice because any other "would be to narrow the potential identification and empathy with the novel's content" (100).

In an interview that appeared in *Quimera* in 1999, Peri Rossi explains that when *Solitario de amor* was published there was a polemic among U.S. scholars because she was using a male narrator. Peri Rossi believes that this polemic was filled with a sense of fanatic injustice "cuando lo que tenemos que reivindicar las mujeres es justamente la libertad que no hemos tenido, pero no para caer en otra opresión" (when what we women should be revindicating is precisely the freedom that we did not enjoy, but not in order to fall into another oppression) (Noñi 13). See Gossy for an excellent analysis of the gender confusion between the female/lesbian author and the male/straight narrator.

4

Self-Reproduction in
El amor es un juego solitario by Esther Tusquets

In advertising, the human body has become so integral that a 1993 article selling lingerie treats the phenomenon in the following manner: "La moda íntima está en plena revolución. La ropa interior ya no se conforma con sugerir sin dejarse ver y cada vez se asoma más al exterior y adquiere protagonismo a la hora de vestir. Con vaqueros, pantalones, los 'bodies' se convierten en prendas habituales en el ropero juvenil" (lingerie is in the midst of a revolution. Lingerie does not conform itself to suggesting without allowing itself to be seen, and every time it appears more it becomes a protagonist when dressing. With jeans, pants, "bodies" turn into customary garments in the closet of the youth) (López de Faro 64). The double meaning of *bodies* confuses the lingerie being sold and the nude body exposed as part of a cultural phenomenon. Bodies, as we have seen in the chapter on *Solitario de amor,* are the protagonists of contemporary ads as they cover product recognition with desire. But desire, as this quote suggests, depends on the definition of *product*—which body is being talked about? In part, pleasure lies in the visual force that transforms one body into another. The advertisement openly invites readers and viewers to take part in a process that, on a textual level, converts bodies of narrative into bodies of consumption. In both literature and advertising, the product relies on the desire it can arouse in consumers.

In Esther Tusquets's *El amor es un juego solitario,* desire depends on the characters' definition of the body as a product. The degree and the definition of the characters' desire is contingent upon how and if they interpret what they see ("Visto y no visto" [Seen and not seen]). An analysis of the use and usefulness of the focalization techniques used in the novel exposes the visual consumer culture at work in the writing of the novel as a whole, in the self-reproduction of each character's *histoire,* and in the formation of the protagonist's conception of his or her own body and sexuality. When *El amor* is analyzed in relation to the forces of visual production, the novel displays the vicissitudes of sexual consumption within the literary game of creation.

El amor begins with an often quoted excerpt from a fictional novel that Elia, the protagonist, is reading. The passage describes the activity of simians in heat; it is filtered through the voice of a young boy who has taken Elia's book and intends to make fun of her by reading the scene to his friends. As the young audience becomes increasingly aware of the erotic content of the passage, they gaze upon Elia as an abject other who resides outside of what they know to be visually—sexually—permissible. As the children imagine previously unexplored worlds of eroticism, Elia becomes the eyes through which others see and read anew. Elia becomes both the object and the subject being looked at. She functions like a lens through which prohibitive worlds can be explored and in which meanings acquire new dimensions. Because the scene intends to enhance the readers' imaginary senses, it reduces the role of the third-person, absent, anonymous narrator of *El amor* and gives way to three centers of consciousness—Elia, Ricardo, and Clara—who serve as the focalizers of the novel.[1] These focalizers tell the story of Elia, a mature woman who is bored with life and searches for fulfillment in fleeting sexual encounters; Ricardo, a young, insecure man who finds his manhood in increasingly overpowering sexual relations with Elia; and Clara, a young woman who falls in love with Elia. Together they form a complex love triangle that discloses each character's past, thoughts, desires, and insecurities in their relationships with one another.

The most noticeable feature of the first pages of *El amor* is the existence of a focalizer whose imaginary capacity projects feelings, thoughts, and actions upon others through the use of perspective and light. From the very beginning, *El amor* emphasizes the importance that focalization plays in the past and present development of each character. In the space of four pages (16–20), the text plays with a multiplicity of viewpoints through one center of consciousness: Elia. Through her, readers encounter Elia looking at herself, Elia peeking in on Ricardo, Ricardo's mother observing Ricardo, Ricardo looking at magazines and imagining Elia, and Ricardo seeing Elia at a party. The text also shows Elia's former lovers looking at her while she is sleeping, Elia imagining a series of male figures, Clara looking at Elia, and others amusingly observing Ricardo as he looks at pornographic material. Focalization, sometimes direct and sometimes indirect, serves to blur the lines between reality and fiction for characters and readers alike.

In another instance, the eye of the camera zooms in on Ricardo's room (16). The room is described as small, with too much furniture and too many curtains, inferring a space of partially hidden, half-uncovered windows into or out of which one can look. The room has books, magazines, and papers strewn all over the floor, suggesting an array of erotic meanings and images hidden in the pages of each text. Curtains and literature imply the inclusion of an observing yet unobserved eye (Elia or Ricardo's mother) that can peek in on Ricardo's actions. As if to tease the curious onlookers, the light goes out, and Ricardo, in the dark, reconstructs Elia, he invents her, and he undresses her (16). In the next scene, at Elia's place, voices of children (perhaps the memories of Elia's past) are heard playing in the school-yard below. Ricardo's "llama" (flame) now turns into a flamelike ray of light that at once directs his sexual fantasies and reflects Elia's own imaginary desires. The rays of light or the focalizers—Ricardo, Elia—move through an open window, along walls and furniture, and pause on Elia's naked body. Here, readers find a "juego lentísimo y sutil de las rayas doradas sobre la piel de un rosa nácar, este cálido sendero de luz, ese aleteo suave y luminoso que se desliza envolvente, acariciante, arrastrándose por la espalda, por los pechos—Elia se despereza y se estremece a su contacto—, por los muslos y el vientre, hasta el vértice de sombra, musgoso y húmedo, al que no habrá de llegar nunca la luz" (slow and subtle game of golden rays on the skin of a rose-colored mother-of-pearl; this warm track of light, this soft and luminous palpitation that slips encircling, caressing, pulling itself along the back, along the breasts—Elia stretches her limbs and trembles at its touch—along the thighs and the belly, to the vertex of darkness, mossy and humid, to where light will never reach) (17).

The parallel rays of light that appear repeatedly throughout these first pages manipulate the observers—Ricardo, Elia's former lovers, Clara, the readers—into visually caressing Elia's body. Elia becomes the center of attention in a process that depends on what Abigail Solomon-Godeau, in a different context, calls the "ideological naturalization of the feminine-as-spectacle, or what Griselda Pollock has called "'woman-as-image,'" that is the precondition for the apparently self-evident homology between the seductive, possessable feminine and the seductive, possessable commodity" (114).

Focalization confuses the identity of both the subjects and the objects. Toward the end of this section, when both Elia and Ricardo masturbate and reach orgasm at what appears to be the same moment, lighting as a narrative mechanism renders the passage's likeness to the complexity of an erotic photograph. The photographic quality of the text confuses centers of consciousness—those of Elia and Ricardo—and increases the imaginary power of the erotic in the eyes of the readers. Readers are left to wonder whether it is they, apart from

Elia and Ricardo, who are to use the scenes played by the characters of *El amor* "para acariciarse con ellas en la oscuridad de la alcoba, para hacerlas rimar una y mil veces en asociaciones infinitas" (to caress themselves with them in the darkness of the bedroom, to make them rhyme one and a thousand times in infinite associations) (19).

Elia is dissatisfied and bored with her life. She needs to create herself and others into images in order to paint herself into a picture or write herself into a meaningful history. Elia searches to place herself at the center of another's visual attention in order to feel alive. To this end, she puts herself in place of the world that surrounds her instead of representing the world to herself. Kaja Silverman, in a discussion of the "mediating role performed by photographic images in our culture" (*Threshold* 197), quotes Jacques Lacan in a passage that echoes Elia's subject creation:

> Images [says Lacan] are meant to render the world accessible and imaginable to man. But, even as they do so, they interpose themselves between man and the world. They are meant to be maps, and they become screens. Instead of pre-senting the world to man, they re-present it, put themselves in place of the world, to the extent that man lives as a function of the images he has produced. He no longer deciphers them, but projects them back into the world "out there" without having deciphered them. The world becomes image-like. (197)

What happens, says Silverman, is that we do not only learn to view the world through a filter, but "we experience ourselves-as-spectacle in relation to it" (*Threshold* 197). We view, she says, ourselves as other.

Elia's desire to be interpellated as other rises from her need to escape the boredom of her life. She searches for "una droga que la libere de la angustia, la modorra, el aburrimiento" (a drug that frees her from anguish, drowsiness, boredom) (92). She desires a drug that does more than provide sexual escapes and lusts after "esta intensidad pues de la imaginación y de los sentidos—sólo remotamente relacionable con el sexo—que constituye la única embriaguez, la única evasión, de la que Elia ha sido desde siempre capaz, desde la infancia ya y seguramente hasta su muerte" (that intensity of imagination and of the senses—only remotely relatable to sex—that constitutes the only intoxication, the only evasion, of which Elia has always been capable since her infancy and probably until her death) (64). This state of being becomes ever more difficult to attain because Elia is bored by her lovers as she is bored by the paintings and sculptures that decorate her house and take on "un aire provisorio, de lugar de paso" (a provisional air, of a place of passage) (49). Ricardo's young, innocent, and pimply face does not fit the frame of Elia's former lovers and therefore functions to give her life story a new twist. Elia includes Ricardo in her narrator as a "poeta invisible" (invisible poet) much like Urraca included Roberto in the telling of her tales. This initially absent third-person narrator can be included in Elia's center of consciousness because "[La vida de Ricardo es] una historia retórica, una sórdida pero al mismo tiempo hermosa página literaria, tan por encima, tan distante el narrador de lo que está desarrollando aunque lo exponga en primera persona, la primera persona no es más aquí que un artilugio literario" ([The life of Ricardo] is a rhetorical story, a simultaneously sordid and beautiful literary page, so superficial, so distant the narrator from that which he develops, even though he may expose it in the first person, the first person is no more than a literary gimmick) (25). The first-person narrator is debased as a narrative technique that allows Elia to include Ricardo's discourse with her own.

Elia needs a new protagonist as well as "oyentes siempre renovados para las historias que recuerda, que fabula o miente" (always new listeners for the stories that she remembers, that she invents or makes up) (93). She chooses Clara to reside on the other end of the narrative chain because "Clara es . . . una oyente fuera de serie, tan atenta, tan sensible, tan respetuosa y receptiva, tan capaz de formular en cada instante la pregunta exacta, la pregunta justa que la lanzará a ella a una nueva andadura del relato" (Clara is . . . an exceptional listener, so attentive, so sensitive, so respectful and receptive, so apt at formulating the right question at each given moment, the perfect question that will throw her into a new gait of her tale) (93). Clara becomes the receiver of Elia's narration (at first indirectly, but then directly as the receiver of Ricardo's narration), similar to the way the readers of *El amor* become involved in the *histoire* of the novel. Elia's text changes through Ricardo's life story and Clara's asserted questions. Consequently, the detested image of Elia looking at herself in the mirror metamorphoses from a bored woman to a nymph, to a wonderful and beautiful being, a virgin, a supreme priestess, and a "Little Queen of the Cats," depending on who Elia projects to be looking at her (80). In other words, she turns into "Elia transfigurada en mito y en emblema" (Elia transformed into myth and symbol) (121) because of the changing intervention of the characters and listeners of her tale. In this sense, Elia's coming into being in a certain shape and form mirrors that of the "Visto y no visto" advertisement for "bodies." Depending on the viewing position of the subject and the object, the definition of the focalized "body" changes.

While Elia often returns to fantasy in order to escape the boredom of her reality, Ricardo includes Elia and Clara in his world of imaginary erotic female figures in order to change his fictional space into a real one. Ricardo's sexual activity consists in gazing from afar. His adolescent sexual experiences are formed by visions of legs, moments of masturbation in his room while looking at erotic literature, and seeing girls—in streets, in bars, and in classrooms—whose bodies he applies to his own invented fantasies (59). When he sees Elia at a party, he realizes that "esta historia que él inventa es asimismo la historia que ella también inventa y quiere, ya que ninguna otra mujer en el mundo—ninguna, ni siquiera Clara, en absoluto Clara—podría ajustarse con tanta precisión e inteligencia, mimar con tales lujos sensitivos, con tantos matices, el papel asignado" (the story that he invents is also the story that she invents and wants, since no other woman in the world—no other, not even Clara, absolutely not Clara—could fit with such perfection and intelligence, pamper with such sensitive luxuries, with such nuances, the assigned role) (36). The fantastic dimension in Ricardo's perception of other women is literalized and demonstrates that "the distinction between art and life is ambiguous, that we understand reality through fictive tropes" (Steiner 71). He meets Elia in the middle of their desired imaginary relations and, according to Elia, begins to caress himself with the letters of her name. Ricardo goes through a process that Wendy Steiner, in a discussion about leftist criticism on pornography, calls "literalist fiction," in other words, the taking of pornography "not just [as] documentary realism but [as] reality as such" (71). The word, *Elia,* becomes real as each letter metamorphoses into the finger of a hand that touches Ricardo's skin. Elia's image and name are taken apart and turned into the letters that redirect Ricardo's sexual experiences.

As Elia and Ricardo get to know each other better and enter a sexual relationship, their centers of consciousness begin to alternate and the narrative changes focalizers. In the early stages, Ricardo is incorporated into Elia's story as a literary page, but as her story begins to include Ricardo and Clara, her text (and image) alters according to the visual images that accompany it. When Elia is seen as "una señora que se aburre" (a woman who is bored) (49) or "una niña perdida, una niña desorientada que busca algún apoyo" (a lost girl, a disoriented girl who looks for support) (35), the consciousness of the viewer changes positions because, as with Ricardo, the image of Elia as a lost little girl "no encaja en la historia ni es compaginable con las imágenes de Elia que Ricardo persigue y mima y colecciona" (does not fit in the story nor is compatible with the image of Elia that Ricardo pursues and pampers and collects) (47). "Compaginable" describes the necessary relationship between what is seen and what may be written on a page. The only way to "hacer compatible una cosa con otra" (make one thing compatible with another)—Elia and Ricardo—as María Moliner defines *compaginar,* is to join each other in the world of fiction (686). When an image changes to the dissatisfaction of the viewer, the story can be altered to harmonize with the version that readers and view-

ers want to see. The focalizers' perception of themselves is therefore always intertwined with the one created by the other "authors."

What Elia and Ricardo perceive as an extraordinary (love) story is for Clara "una aventura turbia, a caballo entre lo sórdido y lo fantástico, entre lo más mezquino y mísero y el más suntuoso ejercicio literario" (a turbid adventure, somewhere between the sordid and the fantastic, between the most wretched and unfortunate and the most magnificent literary exercise) (32). Clara finds the possibility of an "historia" (a sexual relationship) impossible to grasp "porque ¿cómo podía conmover a una mujer como [Elia] una pasión tan torpe, tan literaria, en el peor sentido de la palabra literatura, tan literaria y falsa . . . ?" (because, how could a woman like Elia be moved by such a clumsy, literary, passion, in the worst sense of the word literature, so literary and false?) (58). As the listener to Ricardo's and Elia's texts, Clara becomes the literary critic who considers their story "bad"—perhaps pornographic?—literature because Elia and Ricardo are two incompatible texts. While in the beginning Clara encourages Elia's literary associations in order to help her out of her lethargy, she does not believe, according to Elia, that their relationship could exist as a real story. The jump from *histoire* (a fictional plot) to "historia" is unforeseeable for Clara, who cannot visualize the scenes she is in the process of coauthoring.

Clara's refusal or incapacity to see the sexual dimension that evolves among all three characters has to do with her different approach to the act of imagining. A lack of maternal love is internalized by Clara on the same visual plane on which the erotic images of Elia and Ricardo find their pleasure. When Ricardo calls Clara and gives her minute details about his first sexual encounter with Elia, he provokes the appearance of "una terrible galería de imágenes, imágenes móviles y vivientes, y sabe [Clara] que no podrá borrarlas, que nadie ni nada podrá ya borrarlas durante las largas noches del insomnio, sabe . . . que estas imágenes ingresan, como el desamor de la madre, en ese lugar de la mente o del alma reservado a las heridas irreparables" (a terrible gallery of images, moving and living images, and Clara knows that she is not able to erase them, that nobody nor anything could erase them during the long nights of insomnia, she knows . . . that these images enter, like the indifference of her mother, into that part of the mind or the soul reserved for irreparable wounds) (86). As Ricardo continues to talk to Clara on the phone, his and Elia's bodies turn into a text that he skillfully weaves to increase interest. Yet, in this case, the reaction is opposite to the one he desires. Clara hangs up on him several times, thereby interrupting not only Ricardo's narrative pleasure but also that of the reader's, and his story provokes a gallery of visual images in Clara that create

corporal discomfort "porque [Clara] no puede ni imaginar siquiera—sin unas náuseas intolerables, sin un malestar físico tan intenso que la tiene mareada, aterida, e inmóvil—el cuerpo blando y entresudado del muchacho, su boca anhelosa y babeante e impaciente, sus manos torpes y rudas, sobre la piel tan fina y suave y olorosa a sándalo—una piel lechosa y con múltiples pecas, la piel de una mujer con vocación de pelirroja—" (because Clara can not even imagine—without intolerable nausea, without a physical malaise so intense that she feels seasick, numb, and immobile—the flabby and sweaty body of the boy, his longing, drooling, and impatient mouth, his clumsy and rough hands, on the fine and soft body that smells of sandalwood—a milky skin with multiple freckles, the skin of a woman whose vocation is to be a redhead) (61).

The encounter of the two texts/bodies disagrees with Clara because it displays Ricardo's "progresiva conquista del cuerpo de la mujer" (progressive conquest of the body of the woman) (85)—the moment when the "body-suit" disappears to show total nudity. But Ricardo's discourse also provides a way for Clara to approach the figure that she herself desires. For Clara, the imaginary—and this is why she cannot reside in this space—like love, is not a merging of two identities, two texts, or two bodies, but rather of the division between the two, because "ella se ha manejado siempre en términos de amor y desamor" (she has always handled herself in terms of love and indifference) (57), subject and object, consumer and product. Yet while on one hand Clara rejects the images displayed by Ricardo, on the other hand she is pulled into their seductive web. Within the sexual display of Ricardo's "(des)amor" resides Clara's ideal image of love. The images that insert themselves into Clara's mind are hurtful as well as seductive. The outside listeners—Clara, the readers—are therefore slowly implicated into a narration in which the female erotic affects their senses, and love and distaste are increasingly intertwined.

As Elia's and Ricardo's texts take form, so does the need to introduce an audience. More than a theater piece that has been rehearsed and studied beforehand, their love story can be compared to a real-life performance with a script that evolves during the making. The political and subversive quality of such an act resides in a transgression of appropriate sexual behavior and the psychological effect that the scene can have on its young female viewer. But the subversion of this particular performance must be read in relation to the growing perception that, as Marvin Carlson states, so-called "reality [is] itself experienced only through representation" (174). That is, the reality of Elia's and Ricardo's performance will be perceived by the viewers through the images that they have already internalized.

The repetition of the mirror in different contexts can explain the manner in which the subjects, in this case Elia, visually construct their own performance in relation to their internalized images. The mirror reminds Elia of the "terrible fastidio que le causa su propia imagen" (terrible repugnance that her own image causes) (134) and the "vastedad inconmensurable de parcelas de la realidad que le resultan ajenas" (the incommensurable vastness of parcels of reality that she considers alien) (63). Paradoxically, Elia's room includes an infinite number of mirrors that have one defining factor: their frames are decorated with "pinturas y grabados de mujeres desnudas, dormidas, lánguidas, yacientes, erguidas, espectantes, rodeadas a veces de animales reales o fantásticos, de un amante solícito, de señores con frac y con chistera, con fotos a color de los dos chicos" (paintings and engravings of naked women, sleeping, languid, reclining, raised, spectating, surrounded sometimes by real or fantastic animals, by a solicitous lover, by men in tuxedos and top hats, by color photos of the two youngsters) (127). With a quick movement of the eye, Elia's mirror image can reflect a fantastic animal or a former lover. In the context of the hotel room in which Elia and Ricardo make love for the first time, the mirror helps Elia turn the parodic and grotesque scenery into a performative space (72). This space allows her to view herself in the hands of another: "justo encima de ella, rodeando el espejo más grande de todos los que invaden la habitación, el espejo que reflejará dentro de unos minutos los cuerpos de ellos dos abrazados y desnudos" (just above her, circling the biggest of all mirrors that invade the room, the mirror that in a few minutes will reflect the two embraced and naked bodies) (72). The reason for the mirror, the mirror personified as Clara, and the need for Clara as a real-life spectator is that Elia needs to see herself reflected and valued in the eyes of another. The subversive quality of what Elia and Ricardo construct as a performance lies in a reality based on the value of "I" as "other."

The changing focalizers in *El amor* reflect the game of self-reproduction. Now that Elia and Ricardo's "historia" has points of mutual contact, they must introduce a (present) third person so that they may reconstruct their relationship.[2] Both Elia and Ricardo's "historia sexual" and the *histoire* of *El amor* now disrupt "the private sphere by opening it up to the irrevocable publicity of writing" (Brooks 32). Ricardo insists on filling his tales with visual sexual stimuli in order to increase the imaginary capacity and the reading pleasure of his public. Clara, who cannot stop listening, becomes the target market chosen to be introduced into Ricardo and Elia's private text: "Ricardo la empuja [a Clara] una vez y otra y no permite que aparte su mirada del ojo de la cerradura, la fuerza a ver lo que ocurre en el interior, no bastándole saberla cómplice y queriendo también sentirla espectadora" (Ricardo pushes Clara over and over again and does not allow her to turn her look away from the lock, he forces her to see what happens in the inside, it is not sufficient to know she is his accomplice; he also wants to feel her as a spectator) (46). Clara is pushed to look through a keyhole and into a bedroom. She becomes a voyeur seduced by the voice of an author who is his own promotional manager. Clara becomes not only a viewer but also takes part in the reproduction and dispersion of the text, as does any reader. In the same manner—through a keyhole—readers from the Spanish collection of erotic novels *La sonrisa vertical* are seduced by the book cover through which they can peek and imagine themselves as voyeurs. The erotic dimension of these novels, as well as of Elia and Ricardo's "historia sexual," now includes and demands the existence of a voyeur to make the scenes not only more exciting but also to give them value. *Value* is the key word in a publishing world in which the erotic increases the interest in novels as well as in authors.

The erotic brings the reproduced scenes closer to the public and thereby turns Elia's and Ricardo's performance into a site of consumption. The existence of this commercial dimension is demonstrated when Elia describes Ricardo's feelings toward her in the following manner:

> No es deseo erótico, no, al menos en un primer momento no es precisamente esto. Es como haber mirado durante años y años, años innumerables, los libros o los dulces o los trenes al otro lado del escaparate, más allá del cristal, y que de pronto alguien te agarre de los hombros, los fondillos de los pantalones, y te meta a empellones o a tirones en la tienda, y te diga "agarra lo que quieras, todo es tuyo." . . . Porque Elia es como un escaparate que rebosa prodigios, como una mágica mesa cubierta, bajo la cúpula de luz, de golosinas imposibles y reales, como una bellísima ciudad que se ofrece desnuda a la curiosidad adolescente. (40–41)

> [It is not erotic desire, no, at least not in the first instance it is not precisely that. It is like having looked year after year, innumerable years, at the books or the sweets or the trains on the other side of the shop window, beyond the glass, and all at once someone grabs you by the shoulders, by the seat of your pants, and throws or pushes you into the store, and says to you "take what you want, it is all yours." . . . Because Elia is like a store window that brims with wonders, like a magically set table, under the dome of light, of impossible and real delicacies, like a beautiful city that offers itself naked to the curiosity of the adolescent.]

The relation between Elia and the commodity reflects the idea that "art collapses property and identity, having and being. It is both a commodity and an object beyond price. It is valuable both 'in itself' and as an expression of the culture that produced it" (Steiner 78). Just as Elia juxtaposes the artwork in her home to the consumption of her various lovers, so does her own subjectivity depend on the field of artistic cultural production within which it takes part. Elia's identity gains value when viewed on a commercial level.

The commodification of Elia parallels the narrative strategy of the novel as a whole. The move from one focalizer to another suggests that Elia as well as Clara and Ricardo become (wo)men as images, representations looked at through both male and female eyes. The inclusion of both genders in the objectifying process is essential to the homo- and heterosexual identifications at work in the seduction of the characters and the readers. Clara's homosexual preference is an important aspect of the psychological associations that consumer culture relies on. Diana Fuss, in "Fashion and the Homospectatorial Look," explains that advertisements rely on the desire of heterosexual women to make themselves more appealing to the opposite sex. Fuss believes that by showing "eroticized images of the [male or] female body for the explicit appreciation and consumption by a [same-sex] audience" (713), ads promote a homosexual identification with the "other." Clara's attraction to Elia, through the lens of commodity culture, exemplifies the engendered nature of the industry and allows one to understand why Clara becomes a necessary spectator and actor. The inclusion of Clara is a natural consequence of what Elia calls "bipolar . . . siempre presente Clara en sus encuentros con Ricardo, siempre presente Ricardo en las conversaciones con Clara" (bipolar . . . always present in Clara's encounters with Ricardo, always present in Ricardo's conversatons with Clara) (97). With Clara's inclusion in both Elia's and Ricardo's lives, all characters' relationships move away from simple polar associations.[3]

What the three centers of consciousness suggest, apart from pointing to the solitary game of love, is that eventually all focalizers meld into one-as-other by becoming one another's necessary image of themselves.[4] Each figure becomes part of the other's projected voice: the third person (Clara) becomes the first-person narrator, the first-person narrator (Elia) becomes the third, and so on. Depending on the viewing position, the story takes on different dimensions. Ricardo was the outside third-person narrator who, seduced by his own story, involves himself as the main character. Clara believes that the seemingly innocent Ricardo, whose oral narratives were always well organized, logical, and seductive, planned this "historia sexual" from the very beginning. Ricardo, "paciente y obstinado, en un soberbio juego de inteligencia—¿o acaso sólo de astucia?—, [estaba] fingiendo todos los matices de la pasión y la ternura, en una magistral jugada de ajedrez, y no porque lo amara, sino porque le era necesario para demostrar o para demostrarse—sí, ante todo para demostrarse—algo, y le era imprescindible a Ricardo vencerle, arrastrarla hasta su propio campo de juego, le era imprescindible imponerle su dominio" (patient and obstinate, in a superb game of intelligence—or perhaps only of astuteness?—was pretending all shades of passion and tenderness, in a magisterial play of chess, and not because he loved her, but because it was necessary for him to prove himself—

yes, above all to prove himself—something, and it was essential for Ricardo to conquer her, to pull her into his own playing field, it was essential for him to impose his dominance) (120). The text suggests that his youthful innocence disappears in a manipulated "historia sexual" that ultimately includes both women in its making and slowly positions their narratives on a second and third level.

Following the logic of Ricardo's adolescent visual instead of textual associations, his physical and narrative takeover is related to his desire to fully and literally metamorphose the pornographic female figures of his imaginary encounters into Elia and Clara: "algunas veces las mujeres tenían el rostro de alguna actriz de cine o de la protagonista de una historia porno—, y apareció luego una chiquita con el rostro de Clara, y luego una mujer ninfa que era Elia, y más tarde, hace ya varios días y hasta incluso semanas, surgieron finalmente unidas las dos figuras, las de Elia y Clara, y las escenas pasaron a ser desde entonces a tres, infinitamente sugestivas y variadas" (sometimes the women had the face of some film actress or the protagonist of a porn story— and later a little girl appeared with the face of Clara, and later a woman nymph who was Elia, and then, since a few days ago and even a few weeks, both figures finally appeared united, that of Elia and Clara, and then the scenes turned into threesomes, infinitely suggestive and varied) (133). With the presence of both women, Ricardo can more vividly play out the differing roles of his imaginary female protagonists, but in order to do so he must not only seduce Elia and Clara into his version of the "historia sexual" but also direct each of their actions. It comes as no surprise then that he desires to include Clara into Elia's and his own sexual encounters.

Linda Gould Levine says that Ricardo takes over the plot and reduces Elia to second authorship, thereby making "the male erotic fantasy more imposing than the female one" (211). Levine also states that "Elia has been defined from the start as a voracious and undiscriminating 'consumer' of literature. Nonetheless, she is unable to produce any noteworthy scripts of her own" (209–10). Ricardo can take over the threads of the narrative and make the readers think of words such as *dominance, power,* or *conquest* not because Elia cannot write her own script, but because her script depends on a different system of imaginary significations. For Elia's *histoire* to be written, she must move from being to having, and she must turn herself into the product of another's tale. By contrast, for Ricardo's "historia sexual" to be successful, Elia (and Clara) must become the product of his pornographic readings, in which a product depends on its value in relation to the desire and the imaginary perception of its audience.

In the fluid positions among focalizers lies the clue to the inability to restrict the text to binary associations. In view of Fuss's approach, which includes the "homospectatorial look" in the making of oneself in the eyes of another, all three characters can be evaluated on a visual plane. One character's so-called dominance over the other depends on the other's self-image. For example, when taking into account Ricardo's visual history, the conclusion of his story should come as no surprise if the readers consider that his imaginary system relies on denying "the difference between the metaphorical and the literal" (Steiner 72). The pornographic images of his youth, when read in light of what Steiner calls the "literalism of the left," must necessarily result in a literal reading of images turned action (60). This conclusion can be seen in the author's inclusion of an inexcusably violent and domineering scene in which Ricardo physically abuses and sodomizes Elia:

> y [Ricardo] da vuelta de golpe al cuerpo de la mujer—aquí no manda nadie más que él ahora, ni hay otra voluntad ni otra palabra que la del macho enfurecido en la selva encelada—, da vuelta al cuerpo de la mujer a bruscos tirones, a rudos palmetazos, y le levanta las nalgas, las rodillas de ella hincadas en la sábana, su rostro sepultado en la almohada, y la monta y la cabalga como—está seguro—derribaban y montaban a sus hembras en plena jungla los simios superiores, de espaldas ellas, sin poder los dos mirarse, ni besarse, sin poder hablarse, infinitamente distantes y solitarios, aniquilada la más remota esperanza de comunicación o de ternura, una Elia sin rostro—sólo su cabello rubio desparramado sobre la almohada—, una Elia sin voz. (141)

> [And (Ricardo) suddenly turns the body of the woman around—now nobody but he is in command, nor is their another will nor another word than that of the infuriated male in the heat of the jungle—he turns the body of the woman around with sudden tugs, rough blows, and he lifts up her buttocks, her knees braced on the sheets, her face buried in the pillow, and he mounts her and he rides her like—he is certain—the superior simians who knocked down and mounted their females in the middle of the jungle, from behind, without them being able to look at each other, or kiss each other, without being able to speak to each other, infinitely distant and alone, the most remote hope of communication or tenderness annihilated, an Elia without a face—only her blond hair scattered over the pillow—an Elia without a voice.]

Elia is aware that the success of Ricardo's game depends on his ability to prove to himself "la fuerza de su inteligencia y de su voluntad—acaso su genialidad creadora—, por el método de componer historias vivas, con personajes de carne y hueso" (the strength of his intelligence and his will—perhaps his creative genius—through the method of composing live stories, with people of flesh and bone) (148). The scene demonstrates that this process can only take place by turning Elia into a product without an identity—"una Elia sin rostro" (an Elia without a face)—who can easily be exchanged for the female figures of Ricardo's past pornographic fantasies. Once the seduction of the feminine gives way to a more real, or literal, reading of the object desired for Ricardo, Elia and Clara turn into commodities that have been appropriated and therefore must be consumed/consummated: "used up, absorbed, devoured, destroyed, completed by sexual intercourse, brought to completion" (*Random House College Dictionary,* 1984). That Elia allows Ricardo to use her person to convert his pornographic fiction into violent reality is not a sign of powerlessness or passivity but a manner of self-representation within her own visual system of signification. One does not have to condone his behavior but rather see it as a logical translation of Ricardo's and Elia's aesthetic imaginations.

Elia frames and summarizes the general outlook of the novel when she states that the game will continue "hasta que cese la magia y termine el juego" (until the magic ceases and the game ends) (148). Despite Ricardo's violent act, Elia considers her own imaginary tale successful because the image in the mirror that she despises "ahora parece mágicamente desplazada y abolida, sustituida por otra imagen, aunque precaria, distinta, que ha fabulado tal vez ella misma pero que encuentra magnificada, densa, casi creíble, en los ojos de estos dos adolescentes que la inventan" (seems now magically displaced and abolished, replaced by another image, though precarious and different, which may be self-invented but magnificent, dense, almost credible, in the eyes of those two adolescents who invent her) (148). Elia's system lies in the "virtual power" of her imagination; in other words, for Elia, the visual "appears to provide a particularly intense experience of reality while not belonging to that reality in a straightforward manner" (Steiner 76). What Steiner calls "virtual power" consists in a displacement or confusion of meaning and being without including the literal control that was part of Ricardo's perception of visual translation.[5] Elia's visual game lies in her ability to commodify herself to the fullest. That both Ricardo and Clara included her in their imaginary tales signifies that Elia was successful in representing herself as woman-as-image.

Elia considers Clara, the seeming victim of this "historia sexual," to be the winner of the game even after her disturbing sexual encounter with Ricardo. Elia believes that "Clara la ama, y tiene por lo mismo la mejor parte en el dolor y en la alegría, es en definitiva, concluye Elia, y ahí naufragan y sucumben sus sentimientos de culpa, la que se ha quedado con la mejor parte, la que ha asumido en la farsa el papel más brillante y el más grato" (Clara loves her, and for that reason she has the best part in the pain and the happiness, she is really, Elia concludes, and there her feelings of guilt flounder and succumb, the one who has been left with the best part, the one who in the farce has assumed the most brilliant and the most pleasing role) (149). Clara is the spectator, reader, or listener who has been seduced into the scene. She is the innocent bystander who is pulled in by the erotic quality of the female body that satisfies the fantasies of her imaginary world. She may be compared to the readers—literally characters made out of skin and bones—who, seduced by the plot of the story, are pulled into its narrative thread, its increasingly sexual descriptions, and involuntarily subjected to its psychologically disturbing finale. Ricardo's and Elia's acts linger in the readers' minds and are incorporated into Clara's well of terrible images. But just like Clara, the readers may (try to) leave the scene of the crime and close the book or reread those passages that most attract their interest (or their libido).

The title—*El amor es un juego solitario*—plays with a multitude of meanings: a private game, a game of mirrors, a perverse game, an extravagant and unforeseen game, a free game, a game for two, an almost prohibited game, a game of intelligence, and something more than a game. The game essentially, but not exclusively, implicates the focalization of each character in relation to his or her own set of rules and pleasures. Elia knows that the story that all three of them have created and are performing will continue "porque los juegos como éste sólo terminan cuando los participantes dejan de encontrar en ellos cualquier tipo de compensación o gusto, cuando no queda ya una sola ficha sobre el tablero" (because games like this one only end when the participants stop finding in them any type of compensation or pleasure, when not one piece is left on the game board) (148). The chess metaphor, previously applied to Ricardo, conveys that each player moves in relation to the position of the other with "la ilusión de existir a través del existir de otros, o de sentirse, a través de lo que otro sienta, viva" (the illusion to exist through the existence of others, or to feel through what another feels, lives) (150). The final sexual encounter underscores the paradox of the visual site of self-reproduction out of which a unique value and pleasure arises (Steiner 75). The separate yet intertwining centers of consciousness of the novel create a seductive *histoire*/"historia sexual" that pushes the readers into erotically stimulating and disturbing pleasures of their own. The novel allows the female body to subvert male positions of (sexual) dominance by reappropriating the visual as a field of identification. Translated into a market philosophy, this could mean that despite objectifying and discriminatory practices in the publishing industry, the visual, as a site of multiple significations, may represent a space that can expand the power and the possible positions available to women writers.

Notes

1. Rimmon-Kenan says, in regard to the third-person center of consciousness, that "the centre of consciousness (or 'reflector') is the focalizer, while the user of the third person is the narrator" (73).

2. One might relate the insertion of a third person in the construction of the dual identity of Elia/Ricardo to the appearance of the novel's absent third-person narrator.

3. Many critics base their analyses of Esther Tusquets's novel *El amor es un juego solitario* on binary paradigms. Linda Gould Levine says, "*El amor* crystallizes the building sense of tension between two opposing principles characteristic of patriarchal society: male/female, power/submission, authorial voice/silence" ("Reading" 211). Catherine Bellver considers the motivation for Tusquets's "depiction of the phallus as an instrument of aggression [to be] a desire to portray the heterosexual relationship as an instinctive battle of the sexes patterned on the mating habits of animals. The female is passive, the male active" (17). Stephen Hart states that "both in its emphasis on liquid symbolism and the disruption of binary oppositions, Tusquets's text echoes Irigaray's concept of 'parler femme' as a means of escaping the oppressive laws of phallocentric discourse" (96). Other interpretations fall prey to binary modes of analysis through discussions of female equality and feminist or masculinist readings and writings, a prison that chains critics to the same walls as the text's characters. See Nichols and Vásquez for an extended bibliography of the work of Esther Tusquets.

4. In an interview with Stacey Dolgin, Tusquets answered the question "¿Crees de verdad que el amor es un juego solitario?" (Do you really think that love is a solitary game?) with "Creo que el amor es una historia que te montas tú. Es un cuento que te inventas a ti misma. El otro está contando otro cuento él mismo. Y a lo mejor cuando va muy bien, esto dura tres o cuatro años. Pero... así como se dice que te mueres solo, me parece que amando también amas bastante solo. Aunque el otro te quiera y lleves una vida feliz, es un montaje. Es un montaje muy artificioso el amor... el amor como lo entiendo yo en mis libros" (I think that love is a story that you produce yourself. It is a short story that you invent yourself. The other person is telling his or her own story. And perhaps when things go very well, this can last three or four years. But—just like one says that one dies alone, I think that one also loves alone. Even if the other may love you and you have a happy life, it is a montage. Love is a very artificial montage— love as I understand it in my books) (402).

5. Nina Molinaro believes that "Elia alone senses that all three players have become actors in a drama created especially by and for them, and in so doing, they have insured the reproduction and repetition not of any significant truth but of its simulation. Instead of artificially masking an absent reality . . . , by the last scene the three players refer only to the simulation they have already created" ("Simulacra" 54).

~~~ 5
Sexual Subversion:
Las edades de Lulú by Almudena Grandes

Twelve years after the publication of *Las edades de Lulú* (The Ages of Lulú), Almudena Grandes remembers the changing life experience of winning the 1989 Sonrisa Vertical prize in a newspaper interview entitled "Almudena Grandes: La etiqueta de escritora erótica fue fácil de soportar" (Almudena Grandes: The Label of Erotic Writer Was Easy to Endure) (Ortega Bargueño n.p.). In this exchange, Grandes admits that the publication of *Las edades* turned her life into a fairy tale. The text not only sold more than a million copies and was translated into nineteen languages worldwide, but its success allowed the author to get herself out of a personal and economic rut and to take the first steps toward becoming a professional writer. Since Grandes knew nobody in the literary world and nobody knew her, she presented her book to the prize committee under her real name. The members of the jury, including Juan Marsé and Juan García Hortelano, bet that the author of *Las edades* was a homosexual male about fifty years old. Until the very last moment, says Grandes, they expected her to pronounce the words, "Pero esto lo ha escrito mi tío" (but this was written by my uncle) (ibid.). In an attempt to write a love story with sexual content expressed in colloquial language "que me resultara cómodo, que no me ruborizara" (that would prove comfortable, that would not make me blush) (ibid.), Grandes created a best-selling novel that launched her career and her image into fame, and that disrupted all expectations.

While Grandes was not the first female author of erotic narratives, she was the first female author to have had a significant impact on a large reading audience. Grandes claims that while she is now very much aware of her audience and can foresee public opinion, she wrote *Las edades* with the characteristic

boldness of a first novel bordering on the unconscious, rashness, and ignorance (Ortega Bargueño n.p.). In hindsight, this daring approach opened the
door to the inclusion of a larger number of women writers in the field of erotic
literature. *Las edades* broke new ground on several levels: on a textual level, it
redefined gender studies in the realm of sexuality; on an economic level, it
gained the attention of publishers in regard to the value of erotic texts written by women; and on a promotional level, it highlighted the importance of
the female body in the establishment of a commercial space in the literary
market.

Las edades demonstrates that the female body may be appropriated to adopt
a multiplicity of positions from which to see and to be seen. The female body,
much like in *Solitario de amor,* can resist fetishization and can break out of biologically designated roles at the same time that it is being fixated upon. After
the publication of *Las edades,* the media took the image of Grandes out of her
original context and superimposed it on that of her character Lulú. They did
so in order to heighten the erotic tension of the author and to increase the sales
potential not only of her book but also of their own medium. A similar process
occurs on the book cover of the short story collection *Cuentos eróticos* (Erotic
Short Stories), compiled by one of the most widely read cultural magazines
in Spain, *Qué Leer* (fig. 8). The book presents viewers with the S-like shape
of a female body that brings to mind the Cerámica Zirconio tile advertisement
presented in chapter 3. Both reproduce the female nude cut off from the spectator's vision on the top and the bottom, thus creating an anonymous body
in a pleasing form and a message that can easily be transposed from one
"product" to another. The transfer of one body onto different surfaces presents a visual technique that plays with the power of positioning. The over-
lapping marketing of the author and her text presents the idea that women
writers in the 1990s entered a market economy in which their visual images
were increasingly promoted alongside their literary productions. As such, they
have the opportunity to undermine their traditionally defined (sexual and literary) positions, and they may stare back at their audience through the power
that their images acquire in the mass media.

As Grandes entered the world of literary promotion, she was attributed several identities as journalists, television talk-show hosts, and radio announcers
approached her and her work according to what they thought Grandes's
strongest selling point might be. The writer's image, as was to be expected,
changed according to the chapter or perspective from which the readers of her
work (re)viewed her. "Almudena Grandes: Una escritora con aires de maldita"
(Almudena Grandes: A Damned Writer), "Almudena Grandes. Cocina y vinos
en clave erótica" (Almudena Grandes: Cuisine and Wine in Erotic Code),

Figure 8.   Book cover of *Cuentos eróticos* (Designed by Megastore Creativa, 1998; reprinted with the permission of *Qué Leer*)

"Almudena Grandes: El sexo de los libros" (Almudena Grandes: The Sex of Books), and "Almudena Grandes: 'Jamás he tenido un amante como Lulú'" (Almudena Grandes: I Have Never Had a Lover Like Lulú) are just a few examples. The sexual charge in *Las edades* presented the mass media with an exceptionally appealing marketing tactic. Grandes was presented in advertising campaigns that included published photographs of herself in a bathrobe, lying on her bed, or peeking from behind her bedroom door seductively smiling at the readers. Her sexuality became the center of attention, with headlines that enhanced author-character associations such as "Después de leer tu libro, parece que tu vida ha sido la orgía perpetua: Eres la libertina de este fin de siglo" (After reading your book, it seems like your life has been an everlasting orgy: you are the libertine of the end of this century) (Herrera 56); or "quizá lo mejor que se pueda publicar de Grandes sea algunos capítulos de *Las edades* . . . la identificación de la autora con su personaje es prácticamente constante" (perhaps the best information one could publish about Grandes are a few chapter of *Las edades* . . . the identification of the author with her character is practically constant) ("Almudena" 16).

Seductive images of the author were justified because of her narrative's erotic and pornographic imagery and because of the author's creation of a female character that did not propel mass media stereotypes of womanhood, but established a space for the representation of the "real" Spanish female. Grandes explains:

> muchos lectores y periodistas me han identificado con el personaje basándose en algo tan absurdo como la utilización de la primera persona lo cual es una elección absolutamente libre. Luego yo también incurrí en un error, que tampoco me pesa, que fue dar cuerpo a una mujer identificable físicamente conmigo, al querer romper el arquetipo de mujer rubia y frágil a lo Brigitte Bardot, que es todo lo contrario a mí. Todos estos detalles accesorios han llevado a mucha gente a confundir a Lulú conmigo y, desde luego, Lulú tiene cosas que ver conmigo, pero Lulú no soy yo. (qtd. in Rivas 2)

> [many readers and journalists have identified me with the character, basing that on something as absurd as the use of the first person, which is an absolutely voluntary choice. Later I also made an error, of no bother to me, which was to give body to a woman physically identifiable with me, in order to break with the archetype of the blond and fragile woman à la Brigitte Bardot, who is the opposite of myself. All of these accessory details have led many people to confuse Lulú with me, and certainly, Lulú has some similarities with me, but I am not Lulú].

While the author reiterates that she is only the visual archetype of Lulú, not the sexual one, it is precisely because Grandes is the visual model—or anti-model—that the two women are readily confused. As Grandes and Lulú become intertwined, their voices disappear among the words and images of the reviewers, much like in *El sueño de Venecia*. In fact, one newspaper photograph shows the author holding up her newly published book and smiling under a headline that refers more to her person than to her masterpiece: "¡Una gran Lulú" (A large-scale or great Lulú). For all practical purposes, the publishing house could have just as well used Grandes's face for the cover of the novel. In her attempt to break the barriers that define western female beauty in the late twentieth century, Grandes finds herself trapped in an image that she herself has created. This is an image that sells thousands of copies partly because the exposure of female sexuality is one of the most marketable techniques in the advertising industry and partly because the fictionalized image of Grandes as Lulú suggests the commencement of hyperreal authorships. In contrast to the breakdown of the original in *El sueño de Venecia,* this case "is no longer a question of imitation, nor duplication, nor even parody. It is a question of substituting the signs of the real for the real" (Baudrillard, "Precession" 522). Jean Baudrillard suggests that we live in an "era of simulation [that] is inaugurated by a liquidation of all referentials—worse: with their artificial resurrection in the system of signs, a material more malleable than meaning, in that it lends itself to all systems of equivalences, to all binary oppositions, to all combinatory algebra" (ibid.). The confusion of Grandes and Lulú initiates this process of simulation that ultimately, as in the case of Lucía Etxebarría, buries the true signifier in the empty fiction of its production; it begins to erase the real and replace it with the appearance of a real as presented by the media circus.

The confusion between author and character is propelled by the protagonist, Lulú, who presents readers with reality-founded attributes that reflect a dislocated quality. By "dislocated," I mean the shift of two superimposed images within the text: that of a thirty-three-year-old narrator (who is most often associated with the author) in the present tense and that of a twelve-year-old girl in the past tense, the narrating self and the experiencing self. It is the latter figure that the first-person narrator tries to freeze in time as she tells the story of her experiences growing up and details her sexual encounters with her first lover and future husband, Pablo, and with other men. From the very beginning of the novel, the text presents readers with temporal jumps that move from the adult to the adolescent Lulú. On an average of every five pages, the readers are confronted with the puzzle of an analeptic or a prolepsis that interrupts their complacency. The experiencing self and the narrating self move back and forth and intertwine fleeting moments of midlife depression with scenes of planned and ever more violent sexual encounters: from intercourse to ménage à trois, to fisting, to sadomasochism.

The sudden temporal jumps serve to underline the subject's desire to represent a never aging body and to encapsulate the quality of her adolescent seduction. The power that the pen has in superimposing different moments functions like a knife that performs surgical cuts. In reconstructive and plastic surgery, these cuts are applied to the changing of a nose, the enlarging of breasts, the heightening of cheekbones, or the removing of fat. The pen becomes a symbol for the manipulation of body parts and its use reflects the development of technoscience to enable "a fantastic dream of immortality and control over life and death" (Balsamo 1). Lulú's *Bildung,* or formation, depends on her ability to (sexually) cut her true age off from the narrative temporal flow and to increase the seductive effect of her adolescent figure, that figure which has been lost in time. Seen in this light, *Bildung* as the creation and refinement of a seductive teenage image moves the content of the novel into a sphere of visual appropriation. Through language, the thirty-three-year-old protagonist transforms her body into that of a desirable model-product that ends up mirroring (or simulating) the author.

Lulú's body is defined by a repetition of glances that fixates on its contours while allowing for a free movement of meanings to establish her identity. In the text, the target audience for Lulú-as-object is Pablo, her former husband who finds his ex-wife most attractive as a twelve-year-old schoolgirl. The seduction of Pablo, in the past and the present, occurs through a visual process in which Lulú becomes the main actor in a spectacle that is performed for his eyes only (her implicit audience). Lulú's remembering of the past and recapturing of lost moments by dressing up as a schoolgirl suggests that two terms apply here to describe her visual performance. Lulú plays with the idea of *Verwechsel*—an exchange, a mix-up (Terrell 893), an erroneous interpretation, a mistaking of one person for another, a confusing of a mature woman with an adolescent girl—and a *Blickwechsel* "a quick exchange of glances, a knowing look" (ibid. 151). The *Blickwechsel* highlights the focalization techniques used to increase the book's erotic appeal. In one instance, Pablo returns from Philadelphia to present a conference paper. When he sees Lulú sitting in the front row, the text gives way to a powerful game of glances, looks, and gazes in the space of half a page that highlight the seductive mechanisms at play in the text as a whole. The scene begins by Pablo not noticing Lulú immediately: "Miraba en todas las direcciones con excepción a la mía" (He was looking in all directions except in mine) (145); but as Lulú looks down, she feels his eyes rest on her figure. At this moment, his look turns into a stare and his lips silently pronounce the two syllables of her name. As the protagonist, in a crowded room, slowly strips for Pablo, "dejando al descubierto mi horroroso uniforme marrón del colegio . . . Pablo se [tapa] la cara con una mano, [permanece] así durante unos segundos, y luego [vuelve] a mirarme" (leaving uncovered my horrendous brown uniform from school . . . , Pablo covers his face with a hand, remains this way for a few seconds, and then he looks at me again) (145). Quick glances, mutual exchanges, and hidden and openly admiring looks between the characters include readers in a narrative act of voyeurism that increases the text's erotic charge. The readers are included as the audience of an intimate performance between two people.

The *Blickwechsel* is an in-between look that goes beyond the eye and the male, sexual gaze to language. The act of seeing contains oneself in that of the other, a suturing process of a cut between two codes that searches for feminine identity through its wound, its displeasure. The novel creates an edge between the delight of an erotically charged sex scene and the unrest of an act of sadomasochism. The reason for the production of these edges, says Roland Barthes, in a different context, is because "what pleasure wants is the site of a loss, the seam, the cut, the deflation, the dissolve which seizes the subject in the midst of bliss" (7). As in Lourdes Ortiz's novel *Urraca,* the cut in *Las edades* serves to increase the novel's erotic charge and to reinscribe the protagonist to history.

Blickwechsel takes the readers back to the suturelike coming together of the two edges of the text's discourse (the erotic/pornographic and the bildungsroman) and it discloses the text's cinematic quality. *Suture* is a cut in which the politics of identification are hidden beneath the surface. Suture points to "the process whereby the inadequacy of the subject's position is exposed in order to facilitate (that is, create the desire for) new insertions into a cultural discourse which promises to make good that lack" (Silverman, *Subject* 231). Lack, in the case of Lulú, is defined by the absence of youth, but what is meant by lack on a visual level? In film theory, the camera often works with a technique called shot/reverse shot formation, in which it displaces itself continuously 180 degrees in an attempt to emulate the limited perspective of the naked eye. An example of this is when the camera zooms in on a particular person and then turns 180 degrees to represent the person from whom the perspective was just shown. The process makes the viewers, upon reflection, aware of their own powerlessness because they can see only what is in the frame of the camera and what the person behind the camera wants them to see (viewers are made aware of the limitation of their *Blickwechsel* with the scenes on screen). Cinema tends to hide the true (absent) subject behind the camera and to place a fictional character in the subject's position. This substitution encloses the viewers in the story's fictionality.

In the very first scenes of *Las edades,* Lulú takes on both roles of the shot/reverse shot formation technique. While she watches a pornographic video, she also pretends to be the absent protagonist of the movie as she identifies with the characters and desires to take part in a ménage à trois: "deseé por primera vez estar allí, al otro lado de la pantalla, tocarle, escrutarle, obligarle a levantar la cara y mirarme a los ojos" (for the first time I wanted to be there, on the other side of the screen, to touch him, to examine him, to force him to lift his face and look into my eyes) (10). Readers are included in the process of seeing Lulú see and wanting to be seen. The prohibited character of the video's pornographic content heightens the feeling of the readers' ultimate pleasure because "porn is exciting because of what it offers in terms of 'seeing what we normally do not' and . . . porn films often pay close attention to the narrative techniques of classic Hollywood cinema in which the observer is unobserved" (Mirzoeff 483).

The often studied scene opens the text up to a multiplicity of possible positions at the same time that it embodies these positions within each and every reader. Donna Haraway argues for a redefinition of vision that would allow for the production of what she calls "situated knowledges" (284). Replacing the disembodied "view from above" with the individual "view from somewhere" (292), she emphasizes that "optics is a politics of positioning" (288). The text appropriates, as did Urraca, the idea of the "absent one" (the unidentified eye behind the camera) and places the character and the readers in its position in order to heighten their (narrative) pleasure.

In every novel analyzed in *Contemporary Spanish Women's Narrative and the Publishing Industry,* the female body moves from an object of desire—a painting—to an absent other—the historical Urraca; Aída—an idea of womanhood that resides in the imaginary—to Elia, a fantasy of woman made real. It is not until readers turn the pages of *Las edades* that the body stares back at the spectator in full view. In Grandes's novel, the look replaces "the disembodied view from above" with one that resides within. The focalization technique used in *Las edades* divides the historically censoring eye into an infinite number of perspectives that are determined by the concretization of the female body through mass media techniques. The filmic dimension of the first chapter of the novel represents the idea that "the cinematic apparatus can be considered as a cultural technology for the discipline and management of the human body" and that this "body on film [reveals] things that the eyes themselves [can] not see, using close-ups, and frame enlargements to enhance natural vision" (Mirzoeff 182). An example of how the cinematic character of the novel serves as a foreground for the media's capacity of creation is when Lulú takes the remote control and rewinds the pornographic scene that she is watching: "Intentaba reconstruir la secuencia paso a paso, procurando mantener la cabeza fría y comprenderlo todo bien, seria y atenta como siempre que me planteo una tarea que está por encima de mis capacidades. Quería conocerlos, pero supe renunciar a tiempo. Al fin y al cabo, no eran otra cosa que actores, follaban por dinero" (I was trying to reconstruct the sequence step by step, attempting to keep a cool head and to understand it all well, serious and attentive like I always am when I set forth on a task that is beyond my capabilities. I wanted to get to know them, but I knew to renounce in time. In the end, they were nothing else but actors, they fucked for money) (17). The repetition of events in this passage points to the fictitious inclusion of the viewers, and specifically the female body, in the making of an erotic text "por dinero" (for money). As the description of this pornographic scene ends and Lulú's orgasm fuses with that of the characters on screen, she turns her own life into that of a film or a text and a body to be consumed: "Entonces me ofrecí, era ya como un reflejo" (I then offered myself. I was already like a reflection) (23). The close-ups and changes in cinematic frames described at the beginning of the novel turn into temporal textual cuts that focus in on or distance themselves from various episodes of her life. As the intermediary role of the camera disappears, the novel increasingly includes the look as a tool of erotic pleasure to point to the reembodied image of Lulú on screen and behind the camera.

The full embodiment of vision and, consequently, the appropriation of a multifaceted figure in *Las edades* place the novel on a somewhat different level than the other works in this study. Instead of using the female body to subtly break down the authority of previous systems of writing and viewing, *Las edades* confronts these issues head-on. Grandes places womanhood on center stage and opens the public's vision to spectacular pleasures. The narrator does not stand behind the curtains to watch the show from the sidelines; she appears on stage fully ready to act. In the process of creation, she—the actress, Lulú—stares at her own centerfold: "No recordaba los espejos, sin embargo, las paredes estaban forradas de ellos, espejos que se miraban en otros espejos que a la vez reflejaban otros espejos y en el centro de todos ellos estaba yo, yo con mi espantoso jersey marrón y la falda tableada, yo de frente, yo de espaldas, de perfil, de escorzo" (I did not remember the mirrors; nevertheless, the walls were covered with them, mirrors that looked at themselves in other mirrors while at the same time reflecting other mirrors; and in the center of them all was I, I with my horrendous brown T-shirt and pleated skirt; I face to face, I from behind, in profile, foreshortened) (42).

The succession of poses gives Lulú's narration a photographic dimension that reflects on the consciousness of the taking of her positions. The mirror enables her to look at herself in relation to the scene that is being played out. For example, when Pablo and Lulú first encounter Ely, a transsexual friend, and initiate a ménage à trois, the mirror gives Lulú the lens to set the scene before the action begins:

> Un espejo muy grande, situado exactamente enfrente de nosotros, nos devolvía una imagen casi ridícula. Ely miraba hacia abajo, Pablo fumaba, siguiendo el humo con los ojos, y yo miraba al frente, estaba preocupada de repente, no sabía cómo iba a terminar todo aquello, hasta que empecé a reírme, a reírme estruendosamente yo sola, una risa incontenible, Pablo me preguntó qué pasaba y a duras penas pude articular una respuesta.
> Parece que estamos en la sala de espera de un dentista. (105)

> [A very large mirror, located exactly in front of us, returned an almost ridiculous image. Ely was looking down, Pablo was smoking, following the smoke with his eyes, and I was looking forward. All at once I was worried, I was not sure how all of this was going to end, until I started to laugh, I laughed clamorously, an uncontainable laugh. Pablo asked me what was going on and I could hardly articulate a response.
> We look like we are in a dentist's waiting room.]

Although Lulú desires to sit back and immerse herself as character into the parodic scene, she once again is given control: Pablo says, "la que tiene que hacer algo eres tú, tú te has montado todo esto, tú solita" (the one who has to do something is you, you set this whole thing up, you alone) (106). She decides to take control and begins to act: "Lo cierto es que era yo quien actuaba" (the truth is that it was I who was acting) (106). The sexual scene that follows displays Lulú's role as actor and as director. The text shifts the weight from writing to the importance of creating through action, from product to process.

Las edades plays with the idea of the female body that splits temporal references in order to enhance the changing nature of her image. With every cut and paste, Lulú allows herself more room to maneuver. She adopts different positions (metaphorically and literally) and places herself into the always changing picture of the spectators (Pablo, Ely, the men that she watches, the camera). Her identity develops through the look of the other, but her decision to fetishize herself, fix herself up, into the image that her spectators desire essentially includes the image of herself as having multiple bodies. This divided figure does not provide the clear, unpolitical image of womanhood that feminist critics can joyfully embrace. On the contrary, Lulú proposes a contradictory image of a woman who is not always in control. She is not the director, and she is not the actor/victim of the movie she takes part in and creates; she is both. The novel proposes the importance of taking multiple positions through constant temporal splitting, and the text manifests the role of vision to determine a new position for women writers. As Donna Haraway explains in a different context, "The knowing self is partial in all its guises, never finished, whole, simply there and original; it is always constructed and stitched together imperfectly, and therefore able to join with another, to see together without claiming to be another" (288).

At work in *Las edades* is the concept of *Verwechsel*, an exchange of viewer and character positions and identities that are, indeed, never perfect or complete. In addition, *Blickwechsel* functions to propel these positions on a level that has provoked heated discussions about masculine and feminine agency. Gonzalo Navajas considers the novel's implicit audience to be male, and he believes that "la novela está concebida no para la sexualidad de la mujer—que probablemente rechazaría *in toto* la aproximación del texto—sino sobre todo para una sexualidad masculina estereotipada" (the novel is conceived not for the sexuality of a woman—who in every aspect would most likely reject the approach of the text—but, above all, for a stereotypical masculine sexuality) (386). This claim erases all agency from the sexual energy of the character, the pen of the female author, and the pleasure of the female readers. While women do not have to like the novel's narrative approach or the character's sexual acts, to attribute these realms to masculine sexuality alone (even a stereotypical one), reduces women's voice and choice of "feminine sexuality" (a term built on biologically justified exclusions). On a market level, to say that an advertisement that portrays an erotic female model is made solely for a male audience disregards the point made in the last chapter about the existence of a "homospectatorial look." And while the lines between subject and object may be blurred in *Las edades* as well as in advertising, it is essential to not erase women's visual and verbal agency in the production of meaning. When Navajas says, "la conciencia de Lulú está determinada por un código ajeno a su naturaleza intrínseca: el del receptor masculino de la narración que, aún en su ausencia, sigue estableciendo su predominio" (Lulú's consciousness is determined by a code foreign to her intrinsic nature: that of the masculine receiver of the narration which, even in its absence, continues to establish its predominance) (387), he implies that the masculine gaze does not prize itself only on being all-knowing, all-seeing, and all-powerful, but he forgets that the text's creator and a large part of its readership is female. Lulú is not subject to His supreme existence, but it is He (Navajas, Pablo, the male readers) who, during the act of reading, look through her eyes and look at a woman who delights in being looked at. The power of the *Blickwechsel* in the novel is the reason why *Las edades* should be read in relation to the construction of the look from within the narrative voice without negating or erasing the protagonist's gender.

Las edades, called by one person a "manual de relaciones sexuales" (a manual of sexual relations) (Villamor 46), only (trans)forms those readers who are seduced by its message. For this reason, some feminist critics, such as Silvia Bermúdez, embrace the text as an opening up of women's sexuality, while others, like Barbara Morris and Lou Charnon-Deutsch, reject the text as just another version of patriarchally defined womanhood. Considering that relatively few literary articles have appeared about the book since its publication in 1989 and that the general public has embraced the text with enthusiasm, one can presume that the female body unsettles critics' definition of sexual liberation and representation. When the erotic depends on the agent who does the interpreting, it is the critic's own stare that is made public. While critics must push the text's masturbatory qualities into public light, the mass audience may keep its own lights turned off and the working of its hands to itself.

Even though the readership of erotic narratives in Spain is largely female and the readers of this novel, in particular, are "jóvenes, entre veinticinco y los cuarenta años" (young people, between the ages of twenty-five and forty) (Herrera 57), critics like Morris and Charnon-Deutsch still denounce the novel as subjecting women to patriarchal concepts of sexuality:

> It is our contention that Lulú as literary pornography offers limited critical plurality, for it restricts rather than opens up potential readings and interpretations. The feminist critic of the novel might be seduced by the female author's assumption of a female voice bespeaking female sexual agency that creates the illusion of subverting the forces controlling and containing women's cultural and political representations. Nevertheless, the discursive bind of the novel can be phrased succinctly: it expresses what some women think men's fantasies of women's fantasies are. (303)

While it is undeniable that patriarchal forces dominate cultural society, it is this kind of interpretation, not the novel itself, that closes up the space for women to express (and read about) their sexual fantasies in the realm of hard-core erotica or literary pornography, no matter the form these fantasies might take. Their thesis also subjects all female critics who try to open the text up to a more women-inclusive interpretation to the supposed domination of a male-centered text, thereby leaving women no room to maneuver. And with no room to maneuver, female critics might find themselves with no room at all.[1]

The condition of a mainly female audience and a female author undoubtedly affects the readers' perception of the text. If the author were male, one might be more inclined to accept Morris and Charnon-Deutsch's interpretation. But the author's gender interestingly makes women approach Grandes more readily than men do, even if it is men who ultimately desire to read the novel: "'Suelen acercarse las mujeres, por lo general, enviadas por sus novios, o sus maridos. Si son estos que me vienen con el libro, titubean un poco, se retrasan' [dice Grandes]" (Usually women, sent by their husbands or their boyfriends, approach me. If they [the men] come to me with the book, they hesitate a bit, they slow down) (qtd. in Herrera 58). That women feel more comfortable approaching the author than men do shows that its erotic appeal has opened the doors to a new generation of female readers (while possibly intimidating their curious male counterparts) who do, indeed, at one level or another, identify with the erotic scenes and welcome the sexualized image of the female author.

To interpret the text in relation to women's sexual roles within a patriarchy underscores the project of the novel as a whole, especially when it is read with visual culture in mind. Grandes tries to break down, as many of her contemporaries do, the idea of a gendered mode of writing and believes that one cannot always determine whether a text is written by a man or a woman. Nevertheless, she says, there are authors like "'Henry Miller o Vladimir Nabokov, que escriben desde su sexo porque así lo han decidido'" (Henry Miller or Vladimir Nabokov who write from their gender because they have decided to do so) (qtd. in Herrera 56). She proposes to write from one's sex, not from one's gender: "'En mis páginas, mi sexo se traduce'" (In my pages, my sex is translated) (ibid. 58), and therefore she situates her novel not within "feminine literature" but within what she considers great literature to be: erotic. She claims that every great piece of literature is erotic and believes in the need to "'admitir esa condición de impulso que es el deseo'" (admit this impulsive condition that is desire) (ibid.). Her novel goes beyond gendered identification while not excluding it in the process. Writing and reading through one's sex allow her to go beyond Simone de Beauvoir's "second sex" and include other sexualities in the making. To the question: "'¿Por qué sexo andamos ya?" (What sex are we at?) Grandes responds: "'No sé, yo estoy muy agobiada con eso. El tercero eran los travestís, pero ahora ya empiezan los penes artificiales y tal... O sea, por el cuarto o el quinto. Sospecho que las mujeres que ligan con travestís deben de ser ya el sexto sexo'" (I do not know, I'm burdened by this. The third were the transvestites, but now the artificial penises and such are beginning—in other words, we are at the fourth or fifth. I suspect that women who sleep with transvestites would be the sixth sex) (ibid. 56). Seen from all perspectives, shapes, and forms, from men and women, homosexual, heterosexual, and bisexual, transsexual or transgendered, sexuality has become an all-encompassing vision that rests within the productive forces of visual pleasure and displeasure.

The female erotic has been eagerly appropriated in the publishing industry, from seminude photographs to body parts in bits and pieces, and many types of bodies—Los "cuerpos" de Lulú (the "bodies" of Lulú)—have been offered up to the male and female viewership. Since the gaze/body affects the status of the other (gaze/body), the position of both changes in relation to the next, similar to the way one text may come into existence influenced by the generation of another. *Las edades* opens up new spaces for other female authors, like Mercedes Abad, to work along the same thematic lines. An article in *El País* demonstrates that Grandes's breakthrough is partly the cause of Abad's market visibility: "La segunda edición del libro *Episodios de la vida de Lulú*, título dado en holandés a la obra *Las edades de Lulú*, de la autora española Almudena Grandes, lleva camino de convertirse este invierno en un récord de ventas. Es tal su éxito que la editorial Agathon, traductora, entre otros, de Manuel Vázquez Montalbán y Jorge Semprún, actual ministro de Cultura, piensa lanzar el año próximo en el país a Mercedes Abad, también ganadora del premio de novela erótica 'La Sonrisa Vertical'" (the second edition of the book *Episodes of the Life of Lulú*, the title given in Dutch to the work *Las edades de Lulú* by the Spanish author Almudena Grandes, is on its way to breaking this winter's sales record. Its success is so big that the publishing house Agathon—translator, among others, of Manuel Vázquez Montalbán and Jorge Semprún, present-day minister of culture—is thinking of next year launching Mercedes Abad, also winner of the Vertical Smile Prize for erotic novels) (Ferrer 35).

Through the description of highly erotic and pornographic scenes, Grandes's *Las edades* places the female body where the pleasure of the text meets the displeasure and discomfort of the openly sexual representation of womanhood. This discomfort opens a space in which new women writers can insert themselves and rewrite the canon. *Las edades* differentiates itself from other novels in that the authorial voice of the first-person narrator constructs itself through the lens of her own camera and consciously constructs her own image in the eye of the other. The female body looks back at that which it creates. Lulú (and Grandes) is able to displace herself in time and body through the visual exchange of meanings. A visual analysis of *Las edades* demonstrates that literature written by women cannot continue to be marginalized but must begin to see and be seen from within, with the historical advantage of having seen from below.

Note

1. It is valuable to note that Morris and Charnon-Deutsch do not use the main character's pet name, Lulú, but rather her "adult" name, Marisa. They textually deny the protagonist her imaginary and adolescent dimension.

～ 6
Etxebarría Ecstasy:
The Publishing Industry Exposed

Lucía Etxebarría opens a Pandora's box of literary politics by exposing the motors that make the publishing industry run. She is an author whose outrageous promotional tactics have enchanted and bemused some, angered and alienated others, while gaining the attention of most of the Spanish reading public. My study concludes with Etxebarría not because her work is necessarily the most promising today but because she moves discussion of the female body in narrative to the body (of narrative) in the publishing industry. Etxebarría incites readers' awareness of the role of the female body (as author and character) in the process of creating meaning. She uses her work and her body to increase media attention, promote herself and her feminist messages, decrease the distance between authors and readers, and expose the (discriminatory) practices and politics of the publishing industry. By calling attention to the power of the visual image in positioning oneself in the literary market, the marketing ecstasy over Etxebarría suggests that the industry's marriage to the mass media may result in myriad opportunities.

Etxebarría belongs to the youngest generation of authors in Spain. This group of writers was born between 1960 and 1975 and is variously called Generation X, the Sesame Street Generation, Generation Kronen (based on José Ángel Mañas's 1994 novel *Historias del Kronen* [Stories of the Kronen]), Generation Blank, and Generation J.A.S.P., an acronym that appeared in a Renault Clío car commercial and stands for "Jóven Aunque Sobradamente Preparado" (young but all too prepared). While their topics, styles, and approaches differ, authors such as Gabriela Bustelo, Juan Bonilla, Ismael Grasa, Ray Loriga,

José Ángel Mañas, José Machado, Benjamín Prado, and Care Santos, as well as Etxebarría, manifest sociological perspectives on the lives of twenty- and thirty-something youths. Their testimonials reincarnate the neorealist tradition of the fifties and sixties in a nineties era of violence, drugs, sex, and rock and roll. They speak of Nirvana instead of Vivaldi, they use language that is at times so purposefully raw that it reinvents naturalism, and they create characters that speak of loss, loneliness, and the meaninglessness of life.

Etxebarría is one of the most visible and vocal representatives of this group of authors. Of Galician origin, she was born in Bermeo, in 1966. The youngest of seven children, she attended a Catholic school in Valencia, moved to Madrid at the age of eighteen, received her bachelor's degree in journalism, and worked for a multinational firm. She promoted records, translated books and articles from Spanish into English, and wrote for various publications, including *Ruta 66* (Route 66). In 1996 she published her first book, *Aguanta esto: Una biografía de Courtney Love* (Put Up with This: A Biography of Courtney Love).

In 1997 Etxebarría gained national attention with the publication of her novel *Amor, curiosidad, prozac y dudas* (Love, Curiosity, Prozac, and Doubts). Its creation is an ironic twist of fate; it was initiated because of a love crisis that the author experienced in 1996. On Etxebarría's personal Web page—which is filled with subjective information and questionable facts that mirror her often sarcastic take on life and love—she explains that the person with whom she was living at that time (she does not specify her ex's gender) decides to end their relationship. To relieve her pain, Etxebarría writes this person "una serie de cartas diarias, pequeños cuentos o alegorías de apenas dos páginas en los que iba narrando en tono irónico diferentes aspectos de mi existencia y de las personas que me rodeaban" (a series of daily letters, short stories, or allegories of hardly two pages in length in which I narrated, in an ironic tone, different aspects of my existence and that of the people that surrounded me).[1] After several months of receiving these letters, her former partner asked her to stop sending them. Desperate, explains Etxebarría, she continued to write on her own and translate her surrounding reality into a series of short stories. She then pulled the tales together in such a way that the protagonist of one became the secondary character of another. Based on this model, she finished the draft of a novel, originally entitled *Exceso de testosterona* (Excess of Testosterone), which, one year and eight revisions later, would be known to the public as *Amor, curiosidad, prozac y dudas*.

The cover of *Amor* (fig. 9) easily stands out in stores. It was created by three designers who call themselves "Ipsum Planet" and work with new technologies to illustrate what they call "Oxígenoterapia" (Oxygen therapy).[2] The book cover presents a young woman sprawled in an office chair. She appears to be in

Figure 9.   Book cover of *Amor, curiosidad, prozac y dudas* (1997). (Designed by Judit Commeleran; photograph by Andrea Savini Art Futura; reprinted with the permission of Plaza and Janés Editores, S.A.)

a drug-induced state, her eyes look out into space, and her legs are slightly open for viewers to peek into the triangle of her miniskirt. The illustration is made to reflect a photo negative—a purple figure on a bright orange backdrop. On one level, the cover represents the despair and listlessness of a woman tied to a meaningless and underpaid "McJob"—"a low-pay, low-prestige, low-dignity, low-benefit, no-future job in the service sector" (Coupland 5). On another, more metaphorical level, the cover design points to the negative of a photograph that exposes the story of a woman's deepest secrets. As a negative, the illustration fixates on, frames, or fetishizes that which the naked eye cannot see—the story of not one but three women: the sexually active bartender, Cristina; the closeted lesbian executive, Rosa; and the depressed homemaker and mother, Ana.

In the 1990s, *Amor* became one of the best-selling novels in Spain by a young female writer. The novel's refreshing, colloquial, and humorous style includes references to popular culture (advertisements, magazines, movies, songs), an abundance of anglicisms, and feminist observations, all sprinkled with a good dose of humor and eroticism. The book attracts a large readership and is generally hailed by the literary establishment: "Había en aquella primera obra un torrente de vida y un derroche de autenticidad en su arriesgada exploración dignos del mejor Baroja en sus novelas más encarnadas en la dura lucha por sobrevivir" (In this first work, there was a torrent of life and of lavish authenticity in its risky exploration worthy of the best Baroja in his most embodied novels about the tough fight for survival) (Basanta n.p.). Critics set their sights on this young talent who "empieza por arriba . . . sin complejos ni tabúes" (starts from the top without complexes or taboos) (Vázquez n.p.) and creates what one German newspaper calls a "cyberchic" novel (Von Fries 4). Publishing houses take one look at Etxebarría and smell success: she is a young female author with a best-selling first novel, a marketable appearance, and, above all, a personality that calls for attention.

One year after the publication of *Amor,* Etxebarría received the Nadal Prize for her second novel, *Beatriz y los cuerpos celestes* (Beatriz and the Heavenly Bodies).[3] The novel tells of a young girl, Beatriz, who moves to Edinburgh to find her identity and sexuality. This story rekindles the memories of the character's adolescent homo- and heterosexual awakening as well as the past and the present of her relationship with her family. The novel brings to mind Carmen Laforet's novel *Nada,* which was granted the first Nadal Prize in 1945 (to a then relatively unknown twenty-three-year-old female author). One review, entitled "Otra vez *Nada,*" sarcastically compares *Beatriz* to *Nada* and attacks Etxebarría for colonizing literature with sociology, supplanting opportunity with opportunism, and confusing nihilistic existentialism with mere sentimentalism (Echevarría, "Otra" 11). The subtitle, *Una novela rosa* (A Romance Novel), appropriates the love story, particularly the homosexual love story, as a space for female character formation and presents readers with a queer-bildungsroman. This novel of formation appropriates"nada" (nothingness)—the lack of communication among individuals in a society determined by the abundance of information technology—to define the experience of a generation (Generation X) in search of meaning in the violent, drug-ridden, and fatalistic cities of Madrid and Edinburgh.

Critics complain that the quality of Etxebarría's written word does not deserve a Nadal Prize. Santos Sanz Villanueva claims that "el problema de *Beatriz* . . . no se halla en la observación de la realidad, puesto que sabe anotarla y dotarla de un sentido trágico, sino en su escritura" (the problem with *Beatriz* . . . lies not in its observation of reality, which it knows to note and denote with a sense of tragedy, but with its writing style) (15). Yet a second critic believes that the novel is written in "una prosa sentenciosa y más bien cursi, afín a la que emplean en su mayor parte los reportajes de didáctica sexual, esnobista y sentimental de revistas como *Woman* o *Cosmopolitan*" (a sententious prose that is more or less pretentious and largely used in sentimental didactic reports and snobby, sentimental magazines like *Woman* and *Cosmopolitan*) (Echevarría, "Otra" 11). A third critic says that *Beatriz* "podría confundirse con unas memorias, por el tono personal y por la presencia de ciertos elementos de la realidad que pueden coincidir con la biografía de la escritora" (could be confused with a memoir because of the personal tone and the presence of certain realistic elements that coincide with the biography of the writer) (Masolver Ródenas 35). The novel upsets critics' perception of literary quality and leaves open the possibility that their opinions may be tainted by the body of the writer instead of the narrative body.

When Etxebarría appeared at the fifty-fourth annual reception of the Nadal Prize in 1998, she was dressed in a red outfit, red shoes, red gloves, with a red, heart-shaped bag, and she sported a heart-shaped tattoo on her upper right arm. Her spectatorial image moved her public as much as her critics, who nicknamed her "La reina de corazones" (The queen of hearts).[4] Newspaper articles about the ceremony displayed headlines such as "Lucía Etxebarría: Con ella llegó el escándalo" (Lucía Etxebarría: With Her, Scandal Arrived), "El premio Nadal apuesta por la juventud de Lucía Etxebarría" (The Nadal Prize Bets on the Youth of Lucía Etxebarría), and "Me presenté al Nadal para suavizar la reacción de mis padres a mi novela" (I Presented Myself to the Nadal to Ease My Parents' Reaction to My Novel). One critic went so far that next to a caricature of the author, he expressed his sarcasm in the following manner:

De piedra se quedó mi sobrino de poco más de dos años cuando vio la fotografía de Lucía Etxebarría la reciente ganadora del Premio Nadal. Por el brillo de sus ojos deduje que la personalidad voluptuosa de la escritora casi consigue ocupar el espacio de su idolatrada *Maribel Verdú*. Aquel vestido rojo, pero rojo sangrante, con unos guantes a lo *Gilda*, y un bolso acorazonado que hacía juego con sus pendientes y su tatuaje, le daban un aire *drag queen* sin plataformas . . . que dejó a la mayoría estupefactos. (Lector 25)

[My hardly two-year-old nephew turned to stone when he saw the photograph of Lucía Etxebarría, the latest winner of the Nadal Prize. Because of the glow in his eyes, I inferred that the voluptuous personality of the author was about to take the place of his idol *Maribel Verdú*. That red, bloodred, dress, with *Gilda*-like gloves and a heart-shaped bag that matched her earrings and tattoos gave her a drag queen air without high heels . . . that left most everybody stupefied].

Etxebarría's performance—I dare say costume—increased the outcry not only about her novel but also about the "crisis" of the contemporary publishing industry. Critiques were directed toward a market that searches for authors who have "todos los ingredientes para atraer a todo tipo de lector interesado por las peripecias y la presencia física del autor: del bigote de Dalí hemos llegado a los generosos atributos de una escritora modelo no necesariamente modelo de escritora. Siempre se puede ir un poco más lejos" (all of the ingredients to attract all types of readers interested in the vicissitudes and the physical presence of the author: from Dalí's moustache we have arrived at the generous attributes of a writer-model, not necessarily the model of a writer. One can always take things a bit further) (Masolver Ródenas 35).

Two weeks after receiving the Nadal, Etxebarría did take things a bit further. She appeared nude in a magazine called *Dunia: la aventura de ser mujer* (Dunia: The Adventure of Being a Woman).[5] Her bare body was exposed under the headline "El sexo se aprende, no es una cuestión de medidas" (Sex Is Learned; It Is Not a Question of Measurements) and "Para mi no existe la palabra perversión. Sólo es perversión lo que no me causa placer" (For me the word perversion does not exist. Perversion is only that which does not give me pleasure.) In this risqué interview, which comprises three pages of photographs and one page of written text, she establishes her position in the literary industry by stating that she does not write as a vocation; she writes for money. With these words, she pushes literature from its high pedestal and upsets the egos of several colleagues in the process.

Among other questions from the interview, she answers "¿Y tú con qué artes ligas?" (And you, with what art do you flirt?) with, "Yo ligo con mi simpatía, haciendo reír y pensar a la gente. Con la lengua" (I flirt with my likeability, making people laugh and think. With language/the tongue) (Botana 59). Etxebarría's playful use of the word *lengua* refers to the tongue that kisses, licks, and touches, and to the language she uses to include the physical female body in the narrative thresholds of her texts. Language, in this interview, joins the portrayal of the female body not as a skinny and anorexic-looking super-model—"Estoy harta de este modelo de mujer que nos ofrecen: muchas modelos parecen salidas de un campo de concentración" (I am sick of this model of womanhood that they offer us: many models appear as if they had just left a concentration camp) (ibid. 49)—but as a real Spanish woman. The positions that Etxebarría adopts in these pages remind viewers of the nudes in classical paintings such the "maja desnuda" by Goya discussed in the chapter on *El sueño de Venecia*. Etxebarría's nudes parody the images of female bodies that are used in advertising on a daily basis. One could easily cut and paste the author's face into the "Playmate 1798" ad or manipulate her smile into the Conde de Osborne Brandy ad. While the "Playmate" ad claims that "Si para admirar bellezas como ésta no se conforma con las coloridas páginas de una revista, anímese a verlas personalmente" (If you are not happy with admiring beauties on the colorful pages of magazines, dare to see them yourself), Etxebarría's "ad" and adjoining interview suggest that her image may also be lifted out of the context of the magazine and approached on a level that includes her person in the sale of her product.

When Alicia Botana, the female interviewer, asks Etxebarría what she considers the difference to be between "ser libre y ser libertina" (being free and being libertine), the author replies, "Lo que sucede es que no sé qué es una libertina. Son palabras y denominaciones que no entran en mi vocabulario" (What happens is that I do not know what it means to be a libertine. These are words and denominations that are not part of my vocabulary) (59). By rejecting the existence of the idea of herself as a loose woman, Etxebarría takes her image and the message that she tries to communicate into her own hands. Yet while her linguistic seduction relies on the exclusion of certain concepts and perceptions, her visual seduction builds on a body language that exposes the connotative nature of meaning. The appearance of Etxebarría in *Dunia* makes the author stand on the edge of the imaginary and the real. In a way similar to the promotion of Almudena Grandes's *Las edades de Lulú*, Etxebarría's body is placed in the limelight, and her figure is turned into that of an author-character-model.[6] Her person may now readily be confused with the characters of her texts, and critics may interpret her novels in relation to the representation of the author in the media: "a poco de conocerla se tiene la tentación de confundir el personaje de Cristina [from *Amor, curiosidad, prozac y dudas*] con Lucía" (upon knowing her one falls into the temptation of confusing Christina (from *Amor, curiosidad, prozac y dudas*] with Lucía) (Botana

59). Echoing the words of Almudena Grandes, Etxebarría responds to an author-character confusion with: "No tengo nada que ver con mi personaje. Los tres personajes son estereotipos. Yo quería hacer una novela testimonial y sociológica sobre las mujeres españolas de mi generación, sobre sus luchas, problemas, decepciones. Pero como algunos han visto sólo sexo en la novela, he tenido que poner censura a mi contestador porque no sabes las llamadas que recibo, de tíos y tías cachondos. Pero, yo ni fumo, ni bebo, ni me drogo" (I have nothing to do with my character. The three characters are stereotypes. I wanted to create a testimonial and a sociological novel about Spanish women of my generation, about their fights, problems, deceptions. But since some have been able to see only sex in my novel, I have had to censor my answering machine because you cannot imagine the calls I get from horny men and women. But I do not smoke or drink or use drugs) (ibid. 59). Through the media, Etxebarría has become an eroticized and exemplified version of the young author who is fully aware of the visual power that the female body has in contemporary market politics. The difference between Etxebarría and other writers is that the others are not willing to expose themselves to a mass media with a long history of objectifying female bodies. One could claim that Etxebarría is attempting to reappropriate that space that some have considered "prostituted" or contaminated with female bodies (of narrative).

While Etxebarría's first novel establishes her writing career and her image as a young, twenty-something, natural-looking young woman, the photograph on her subsequent novels exhibits a radical change in appearance. On the jacket of *Beatriz,* we see a woman who has makeup on her face and polish on her nails. She wears a variety of rings on her fingers, a heart-shaped necklace, and a black dress with fluffy edges that reminds one of Hollywood movie stars in nightgowns. After *Beatriz,* Etxebarría—in Madonna-like fashion—began to change her image on a regular basis in order to increase her newsworthiness. In one instance, she is seen walking around town in overalls, surrounded by a number of transsexual and androgynous friends. On the cover of the May 1998 issue of one of the most widely read literary (gossip) magazines in the country, *Qué Leer,* Etxebarría is shown in a black suit and a golden blouse, with her dark hair slicked back against her head, her eyes looking straight at the viewers, and a cigar in between her fingertips (reminiscent of the Lewinsky affair).[7] In the magazine, the author exchanges the cigar for a red rose, and her image is accompanied by the words: "Editorial Destino nos la puso la noche de Reyes como un regalito envuelto en seda roja para que nos caldease el crudo invierno literario. Algunas malas lenguas dicen que ha sido un regalo envenenado, pero la última palabra la tienen los lectores y de momento *Beatriz y los cuerpos celestes* (Destino) ya lleva casi 100,000 ejemplares vendidos" (Des-

tino [the publishing house] gave her to us on the evening of the Twelfth Night like a present wrapped in red silk so that she would warm up the harsh literary winter. Some mean tongues say that she has been a poisonous present, but readers have the last word and right now *Beatriz y los cuerpos celestes* [Destino] has already sold more than 100,000 copies) (*Qué Leer,* May 1998, 92). The photograph of Etxebarría shows an author who is staring directly into the eyes of the beholders. The ironic, Mona Lisa–like position of her upper lips seems to indicate that she knows whether she was indeed a Christmas present wrapped in red silk or one dipped in red poison.

Etxebarría's conscious appropriation and discussion of the publishing industry becomes apparent outright in her third book, *Nosotras que no somos como las demás* (We Who Are Not Like the Rest of Them), published in 1999 by Destino. In this text, Etxebarría pulls together a series of short stories that had appeared in various media over the previous two years. These stories, characterized by their "video clip" quality—short, visual, and seductive—read as a novel about four women who, according to the author, "se sedujeron, intercambiaron experiencias, siguieron adelante... y al final, creo, optaron por abandonarme y se marcharon en busca de un lugar más confortable, mejor ventilado, menos negro que el universo de mis fantasías" (they seduced one another, they interchanged experiences, they continued forward—and in the end, I think, they opted to abandon me and so they left in search for a more comfortable, better ventilated, and less black universe than my fantasies) (10). More important than the stories of these characters is the way Etxebarría uses the prologue as a political space. Etxebarría fills the first few pages with a discussion of women's rights. She uses statistical and sociological information to send a strong feminist message, and she concludes with a call for action:

algunas mujeres no nos conformamos con trabajos infravalorados, infrapagados o no pagados en absoluto. Algunas mujeres estamos hartas de que nuestro aspecto importe más que nuestras acciones. Algunas mujeres no admitimos que nos llamen ninfómanas si demostramos nuestros intereses sexuales o lesbianas cuando reclamamos nuestro derecho a no satisfacer por imposición los de otros. A algunas mujeres no nos gusta que se cuestione nuestra decisión de vivir solas aduciendo que hemos sido incapaces de encontrar hombre de verdad. Algunas mujeres reclamamos salarios iguales y guarderías subvencionadas. . . .

Algunas mujeres protestamos.

Y a estas mujeres está dedicado este libro.

Some women do not resign ourselves to work that is undervalued, underpayed, or not payed at all. Some women are sick of the fact that our appearances are more important than our actions. Some women do not accept being called nymphomaniacs if we demonstrate our sexual or lesbian interests, when we

claim our right to not satisfy, by imposition, that of others. Some women do not appreciate that our decision to live alone is questioned with claims that we have been unable to find a real man. Some women demand equal salaries and subsidized day care. . . .
Some women protest.
This book is dedicated to those women.]

This dedication contributes to Etxebarría's inclusion of comments (by herself and through her characters) of issues pertaining to female sexuality, women in society, and women in literature. Her feminist opinions, scattered throughout her work, add to the polarization of the reception of her enterprise.

Rosa Montero explains that the fifty years of the European feminist movement is reduced, in the case of Spain, into three decades, from the 1970s to 2000. As such, the reaction to and against feminism is likely to be summed up by the divide between those older than fifty and those younger than fifty. Considering that the largest readership of contemporary narratives ranges from sixteen to forty-four years old, it is perhaps not surprising that this age group reacts in a positive yet reserved manner toward Etxebarría's viewpoints. Montero states that since the Spanish feminist movement did not enter Spain until the 1970s, activist groups were never very strong, the analytical and theoretical production has been meager, and feminist print has not had a significant social impact. On the other hand, the Instituto de la Mujer, academic departments committed to women's studies, and women's bookstores, such as Librería de Mujeres in Zaragoza and Librería Sal de Casa in Valencia, have contributed to social and cultural gender studies and the dissemination, financing, and awarding of prizes to literature written by women. These venues, nevertheless, have been claimed "radical" and rejected by the general public. For all of these reasons, the term *feminism* has not been embraced as a term for self-definition (Montero, "Silent Revolution" 381–83).

Some critics thus include comments such as the following in their evaluation of Etxebarría's work: "Lucía Etxebarría muestra su capacidad tanto para la construcción de escenas como para deslizarse por terrenos eróticos. El resultado es un universo narrativo original y personal al que en ocasiones perjudica su explícita beligerancia feminista" (Lucía Etxebarría demonstrates that she has talent to construct scenes as well as slip into erotic terrain. The result is a narrative universe that is original and personal but at times harmed by her explicit feminist belligerence) (Martín xxi).

After her politically charged dedication in *Nosotras* that ends the section called "No son como los demás..." (They are not like the rest—), Etxebarría explains the origin of her various short stories and sheds light on humorous episodes in each instance. In one case, she talks about having to follow the impossible requirements of an editor, whom she ironically calls "La Misión del Poder en la Sombra" (The Mission of the Power in the Shadows), and who asks her to "escribir un relato que tuviera exactamente cuarenta y dos páginas—ni una más ni una menos—, divididas en seis entregas de siete páginas cada una. Cada una debía constituir una entidad en sí misma, como un subcuento dentro de un cuento. Y el trabajo debía entregarse en quince días, sin retrasos" (to write an account that would include exactly forty-two pages—no more, no less—divided into six installments. Each one was to constitute an entity in itself, like a story within a story. And the work was to be delivered in fifteen days, without delay) (11). Her reaction—"Pero eso es imposible, Miguel" (But that is impossible, Miguel)—is modified to "¿Quién ha dicho imposible?" (Who said impossible?) upon learning the amount of pay. On another occasion, Etxebarría talks about a story that her friends consider "lento y aburrido (por no decir intragable)" (slow and boring [not to mention unbearable]) and she gives the readers her "permiso explícito para leerlo en diagonal, siempre que lo lea, pues si no no podrá comprender detalles del resto del libro" (explicit permission to read it diagonally, as long as you read it, for if you do not, you will not be able to understand some of the details from the rest of the book (19). She also gives the Web address of a sex-toy company called Goodvibes, where one of her stories apparently first appeared, and, most importantly, she gives the address of her own Web page (changed since the publication of *Nosotras*). At this Web site, viewers can learn about her "true" life story: "Nací en el año de gracia de 1966. En la tierna juventud fui secuestrada en Marruecos por un tratante de blancas, que me canjeó a mi entonces novio por tres camellos y una bola de hachís" (I was born in the graceful year of 1966. In my tender youth, I was kidnapped in Morocco by a dealer of white women who traded me from my then boyfriend for three camels and a ball of hashish). At the Web site, readers can indulge in several pieces of Etxebarría's poetry; learn about her favorite actors, movies, and books; see a picture of her dog, Cuca; admire her altars of hearts; read about the effects of various drugs; and learn about her first three novels. Onlookers can see personal images of Etxebarría and write a personal message to the queen of hearts. More important than the information that Etxebarría publicizes is that readers enter a new kind of relationship with the traditionally absent author. Here the author is at the fingertips of the readers and is accessible in terms of communication and revealing her own psychology.

Etxebarría uses the prologue in *Nosotras* to redefine the role and position of (female) authors in the twenty-first century. As the Internet shrinks the space between writers and readers and blurs the lines between artforms, Etxebarría has turned herself into a source of erotic self-promotion. In the process, she has turned her texts inside out to create what one critic considers a "visión feminista y denuncia a través de una estética de anuncio publicitario lo que no le gusta del mundo, lo que a sus ojos no es como debería ser" (a feminist vision and denunciation through the aesthetic of an advertisement of her dislikes of the world and of what, in her eyes, is not how it should be) (Bengoa 56). In other words, she exposes the politics, workings, and power of the market in her prologue and appropriates the industry before it appropriates her: "'la aparición de una industria editorial potente proporciona al escritor un doble juego: o se lo comen o puede utilizar el sistema para luchar contra el sistema. . . . [Yo] me aprovecho del sistema; si tengo la oportunidad de llegar a 30,000 personas—como ya he llegado con la tercera edición de [*Nosotras que no somos como las demás*]—... aprovecho la oportunidad para hacerlo'" (the appearance of a powerful publishing industry provides writers with a double-edged game: the system eats them alive or they use the system to fight against the system. . . . [I] take advantage of the system; if I have the opportunity to reach 30,000 people—as I have already done with the third edition of [*Nosotras que no somos como las demás*]—... I take advantage of the opportunity to do so) (qtd. in Arnaiz 63).

Etxebarría is very much aware of the changing characteristics of the publishing industry and of her position in that institutional framework. With the publication of each novel, her voice and image surface. In *Amor,* she is all but a name that defines a new novel on the market. In *Beatriz,* her "Gilda-like" appearance at the Nadal reception gives her as much fame as her discourse does. In *Nosotras,* Etxebarría's personal opinions, if read, define the prologue and preempt the stories. In addition, the neon pink cover (fig. 10) calls the attention of the readers and displays a woman in a position that is reminiscent of James Bond or Charlie's Angels characters. When one looks closely at the book cover, one can see that the woman is Etxebarría herself, dressed in a sexy, tight leather outfit, and drilling a hole into that heart that has come to define her. In a newspaper interview, Etxebarría admits that the text, which "se carga todas las reglas de la novela" (throws all narrative rules out the window), could not have been published if she had not won the Nadal Prize one year earlier. She uses her fame to launch a series of short stories, spread her feminist discourse, and expose some of the politics of the publishing industry.

Time will tell whether Etxebarría's image will slip away and leave only her marketing presence in the memory of literary critics. In the meantime, she has published a book that seems to have grown out of the need to react directly to the demands, questions, and pressures of the literary establishment. In April 2000 Etxebarría published a text that includes two sections that read more like a personal defense diary and a sociological dissertation than a novelistic

Figure 10.   Book cover of *Nosotras que no somos como las demás* (1999). (Designed by Pablo San José; photograph by Martín Sampedro; reprinted with the permission of Editoria Destino, S.A.)

enterprise. Riding on the idea of a new generation of women writers who are daughters of Eve "pero [herederas] de Lilith" (but heirs of Lilith) (Botana 59), Etxebarría publishes a dual-natured text. The first side of the book is called *La Eva futura: cómo seremos las mujeres del siglo XXI y en qué mundo nos tocará vivir*. (The Future Eve: How We, the Future Women of the Twenty-First Century Will Be and in What Kind of a World We Will Have to Live in). The cover, once again designed by Pablo San José, shows a collage of a woman in a slick blue bodysuit—reminiscient of Fritz Lang's female protagonist in the movie *Metropolis*—whose voluptuous breasts dominate the beholders' vision. The woman stares at a rainbow-colored apple in her right hand, reminiscent of Douglas Coupland's definition of underpaid and overworked "McJobs." In contrast to the bright pop-art colors of the bodysuit, her hand and her face display real-life colors and features that make the viewers look twice to see whether Etxebarría herself has been cut into the design. On the inner jacket of this book, the author is once again dressed to seduce in white feathers and heavy makeup, and on the book's jacket the text and the image complement each other in a playful succession of ideas: "En un mundo artificial, contaminado, en el que las estructuras familiares se desintegran, los alimentos se manipulan genéticamente, la realidad se traslada a un universo virtual, las relaciones personales son cada vez más violentas y sólo los bits perduran, ¿quiénes somos, de dónde venimos y adónde vamos las mujeres del tercer milenio?" (In an artificial world, contaminated, in which family structures are disintegrating, food is genetically altered, reality is transferred to the virtual universe, interpersonal relations are increasingly more violent, and only bits last, who are we? Where do we come from and where are the women of the third millennium going?).

Etxebarría explains that the title, *La Eva futura*, is taken from a novel by Auguste de Villiers de L'Isle-Adam published in 1885. This novel was written "en forma de folletín por entregas, en la que narraba el intento de crear una mujer artificial hecha a medida de los deseos de los protagonistas" (in the form of a serial in which he narrated the attempt to create an artificial woman made to the measurements and the desires of the protagonists) (Etxebarría, *Nosotras* n.p.). The intention of the author is to reappropriate this title from a perspective that gives voice to three distinct chapters: "¿Quiénes somos?" (Who are we?), "¿De dónde venimos?" (Where are we coming from?), and "¿A dónde vamos?" (Where are we going?). In these sections, she discusses everything from homosexuality, religion, domestic violence, and the image of women in the mass media, to women's rights after the Lewinsky affair, the sexism of the Spanish monarchy, and Valentine's Day, among other topics. She even includes an addendum called "El test Etxebarría: ¿Eres una mujer desesperada?"

(The Etxebarría Test: Are You a Desperate Woman?). This exam is directed, she says, exclusively at readers who are single and older than 25 years of age. Based on a system of points that one can accumulate by answering yes or no to questions such as "No sé si el amor compensa el sufrimiento o es el sufrimiento el que compensa el sufrimiento" (I do not know whether love compensates suffering or it is suffering that compensates suffering), the results determine whether one is a lost case or whether there is a future beyond one's life as a single woman. The outcome of the test is described in a humorous, and oftentimes ridiculous, style.

In an interview that followed the publication of *La Eva futura*, Etxebarría stated that her intention was not to create an academic text. She was not interested in including an extensive bibliography, and she wanted the book to target a general female audience, not an academic one. The term *feminism*, says Etxebarría, alienates many people in Spain, since it is too academic and it has been rejected as being too radical. Feminist essays are often too difficult to read, have a limited distribution, and are targeted at the academic community. Etxebarría wanted to produce a text that was easy to read, for a public that normally does not read about feminism. *La Eva futura*, says Etxebarría, is for those young Spanish women who often reject calling themselves "feminists," but whose discourses are saturated with equal rights demands (Fraile n.p.). Etxebarría becomes the "popular feminist" by wrapping her discourse into a novelistic genre and by taking advantage of her stardom to reach millions of readers. It is perhaps precisely because of her feminist platform that Etxebarría is more appreciated in the academic world outside of Spain.

In reaction to Etxebarría's contested position in the Spanish literary market, the other side of the book—when it is turned around and upside down—presents another separate but joined text called *La letra futura: El dedo en la llaga, cuestiones sobre arte, literatura, creación y crítica* (The Future Letter: The Finger in the Flame, Questions about Art, Literature, Creation, and Criticism). Here, Etxebarría pulls together her sometimes conflicting views regarding women's rights and women in the market. The book jumps from one topic to another in an attempt to defend her actions as a person and as an author in a style that is supposed to be critical, but more often than not falls into conversational gossip and defensive discourse. The cover displays a Yield sign with a fountain pen icon on it, perhaps to present the systems, people, and connections to which contemporary authors must yield in their attempts to publish. The inside of the jacket carries a photo of Etxebarría dressed in black with her hair flowing naturally in the wind. The copy underneath the image proclaims that this section of the book is about "Todo lo que usted siempre quiso saber y nunca se atrevió a preguntar sobre los entresijos del mundillo literario

revelado por una de las plumas más cáusticas de la joven narrativa española"
(Everything you always wanted to know about the secrets of the literary world,
and never had the guts to ask, uncovered by one of the most caustic pens of
young Spanish narrative). The promotional summary contradicts itself by presenting a gossip column wrapped in a critical argument. While neither one
of the books-in-one may increase Etxebarría's standing in the eyes of the literary establishment, and has been criticized for its "yo-ismo" (egocentrism),
the author once again surprises her public. Not only are readers surprised by
her candid exposition of personal ideas and strong feminist stances, but after
reading a few chapters of the book and turning off the light in the room, readers' eyes adjust to the darkness and discover that the latest book by Etxebarría glows in the dark.

What becomes clear in the context of a marketing analysis of Etxebarría is
that the author plays with her appearance much like the painting is played
with in *El sueño de Venecia*. With each chapter in Etxebarría's career, she alters—cuts, pushes, covers, or paints over—her image and her position in the
market. With the publication of every book, she undermines the verbal and
brings to the forefront the importance of the visual in an increasingly com-
petitive publishing industry. The true *Urkunde*—the text, not the image—becomes ever more buried in the marketing gimmicks that she uses to claim
the attention of her public. In Paloma Díaz-Mas's novel, the visual—the painting—gives the textual—each chapter's interpretation of the painting—a newly
identified body of narrative. It undermines the authority of the original and
emphasizes the metamorphosing position of the work of art within the field
that authorizes it. In the case of Etxebarría, the female body shifts the emphasis
of origin from the verbal to the visual that resides *outside* of the text. Etxebarría could truly be the missing sixth chapter of *El sueño de Venecia* (instead
of the sixth chapter of *Contemporary Spanish Women's Narrative and the Publishing Industry*). She could very well step out of the mysterious painting of
Doña Gracia and make fun—as she does in *La letra futura*—of the voice of
the academic narrators and the institutional network that gives value to the
work of women in the arts.

The authority of the literary establishment that Etxebarría undermines, in
conjunction with a strong feminist stance, is reminiscent of the ideas presented
in the other five chapters of this study. The appearance of Etxebarría's nude
images in the Spanish magazine *Dunia* brings to mind the sculpture of Urraca
in the church as a sign of the adulterous queen. Urraca demonstrates that by
claiming her right to rewrite history, she regains the ability to reposition her
image in light of her own perspective. Etxebarría repositions the image of the
female author at the end of the millennium. To some, she prostitutes women

writers and reduces them to Lulú-like dolls; to others, she liberates and opens the doors to a more inclusive representation of texts written by women (with every look readers see a repositioned Etxebarría). She is loved by the public and rejected by the critical establishment. Women writers abhor the marketing gimmicks that she uses to call attention to herself because they contribute to the sexist and marginalizing characterization of women writers, and because her tactics distort promotional expectations. Regarding the effect that Etxebarría has on the literary world, Laura Freixas believes that, "su trayectoria ha contribuido a aumentar el interés de los editores hacia las escritoras (luego me enteré de que en la Feria de Frankfurt se ha acuñado una expresión: angry young women, y cada editor intenta tener la suya) pero también a desprestigiarlas" (her trajectory has contributed to increasing the interest that publishers have toward women writers [later I found out that at the book fair in Frankfurt an expression was coined: angry young women, and every publisher tries to have his or her own] but also to discredit them) (e-mail message, 5 Aug. 2000).

This particular, perhaps angry young woman, in contrast to the voiceless female lover of the protagonist in Cristina Peri Rossi's *Solitario de amor,* has had the courage to open the silenced lips of the literary establishment in Spain—of authors, critics, and publishers alike. She demonstrates that the use of the female (erotic) body increases the attention that is given to women's bodies of narrative. She also proves that while women have been traditionally objectified in the visual arts and particularly in the mass media, there is, as shown in Esther Tusquets's novel *El amor es un juego solitario,* another way to see and to be seen. Whether she is hated by some or loved by others, whether she is considered a menace to the advancement of texts written by women or propels their visibility, Etxebarría exposes the system that determines the value of works written by female authors.

Notes

1. The personal Web page that Etxebarría advertised in her book *Nosotras que no somos como las demás* is <http://www.teleline.es/personal/luciaetx>. Since then, her Web page address has changed to <http://www.clubcultura.com/clubliteratura/clubescritores /luciaetxebarria>.

2. The "Ipsum Planet" group includes the designers Javier Abio, Ramón Fano, and Rubén Manrique. They appeared on the scene in 1994 and worked for advertising giants such as DMB&B, Walter Thompson, Tiempo BBDO, Bassat, Ogilvy & Mather, Teleline, Frame Relay, Fanta, Burger King, and Ariola. In 1995 they chartered the publication *Neomanía,* which they define as "un espacio abierto a la experimentación visual y divulgación de nuevas tendencias culturales" (a space open for visual experi-

mentation and the dissemination of new cultural tendencies) (<http://www.bitniks.es /WHO/1996/ipsum.shtml>).

3. Etxebarría was awarded three million pesetas for the Nadal Prize. The prize-selection committee included Pere Gimferrer, Jorge Semprún, Rosa Regás, Andreu Teixidor de Ventós, and Antonio Vilanova (Moret, "La joven" 28). It is rumored that her novel was contracted by Destino for the Nadal Prize. Etxebarría chose the title *Beatriz y los cuerpos celestes* because, "En todo el libro hay una especie de cosmogonía y me gustaba la metáfora de la órbita cementerio, que es una órbita espacial adonde van a parar todos los satélites que ya no sirven. Me parecía una imagen preciosa, muy poética y muy adecuada para mi protagonista, que vive en un mundo de comunicaciones fracasadas y de gente que da vueltas sin relacionarse los unos con los otros" (In the entire book there is a kind of cosmology. I liked the metaphor of the cemetery orbit, which is a spatial orbit where all of the satellites that do not work anymore end up. I found the image lovely, very poetic and very adequate for my protagonist, who lives in a world of failed communications and people who circle one another without relating to each other) (Moret, "Me presenté" 28).

4. Etxebarría later denounced the outcry that her red outfit produced and claimed that the dress she wore was the only party dress she owned at the time (Ballarín 28).

5. The magazine *Dunia* is no longer in existence.

6. Etxebarría states: "Almudena Grandes abrió un poco el camino y yo lo abro un poco más a las que vengan detrás" (Almudena Grandes opened the path a bit, and I am opening it a bit further for those who come after me) (Vidal 45).

7. The Lewinsky affair, also known as the Lewinsky scandal, became front-page news for several months during former U.S. president Bill Clinton's second term (1996–2000). Monica Lewinsky was a White House intern who, while speaking to Linda Tripp over the phone and on tape, admitted to having an affair with Clinton. While under oath, she initially denied the affair, but later changed her testimony to prevent prosecution. The former president initially denied the allegations but had to admit to the relationship after DNA testing on a dress from Lewinsky confirmed his identity. When Clinton, before a court of law, had to defend himself against accusations of perjury and obstruction of justice he had to describe, in detail, the extent of his physical contact with Lewinsky. One of these interactions with the intern includes the use of a cigar that Clinton supposedly introduced into Lewinsky during an intimate moment. The cigar episode became a national joke.

7

Autobiographical Sketches:
Female Authors Speak Out

The ecstasy surrounding Lucía Etxebarría's appropriation and exposition of the book market makes us question the power that women writers have to bring themselves fame and seduce their audiences without objectifying themselves in the process or reducing the quality or political philosophy of their literature. The same seduction or horror that is used to attract buyers and mold the image of female authors (as hysteric, not worthy, seductive, classic), as well as the discriminatory practices that reduce novels written by women to the attraction of their actual bodies, can be appropriated by authors as a force to undermine the dominant structure. In other words, women writers can use the seductive power of the female image to undermine the field that has reduced their bodies to their sexual appeal. When Etxebarría, after accepting the Nadal Prize, posed nude, she (perhaps unknowingly) lifted the seductive power of the female body out of its literary context and turned the forces of the market into a parodic site of discussion. By doing so, she pulled the rug out from under those critics who cannot separate a female writer's body from her text. Etxebarría demonstrates that the production of women writers in Spain is closely linked to their ability to function within and take advantage of the forces that constitute the literary market.

The question that remains to be answered is to what degree authors actually change their positions and their production in light of the (visual) forces of the publishing industry. It is logical, then, to conclude this book with a section that gives women writers the power to comment on their own experiences in the literary market. As an extension of earlier chapters, the following pages give testimony to several known and lesser-known writers from various generations, including Paloma Díaz-Mas, Rosa Montero, Clara Obligado, Marta Sanz, Lola Beccaria, Paula Izquierdo, Care Santos, and Espido Freire. In letters and e-mail messages that I exchanged with the authors since 1997 and in personal interviews conducted in the summer of 2000, the women comment on the degree to which the industry has had an effect on their professional lives. The writers answer questions such as the following: "In what way does the market affect the production of your texts?" "How are your books promoted?" "What difficulties have you encountered when dealing with the literary market?" "Do you believe that gender is a factor in the marketing and the reception of your works?" Each author answers these questions to varying degrees. Their insights make apparent that according to an individual writer's character, background, and financial and personal situation, each author reacts in relation to the set of forces—political, economic, social, popular—that determine the cultural production of the literary field at a particular time in their personal histories. They expand on the project of this book by highlighting the importance of their personal histories vis-à-vis the publication, dissemination, and reception of their novelistic enterprise.

Paloma Díaz-Mas (b. 1954 in Madrid)

Paloma Díaz-Mas largely works independently of the demands of the market. She is a professor in the department of literature at the Consejo Superior de Investigaciones Científicas in Madrid. She works without an agent but with the publishing house Anagrama of Barcelona, a medium-sized business headed by Jorge Herralde. Anagrama has resisted takeover by multinational firms and has kept alive its reputation of high literary standards and creative freedom. Díaz-Mas recognizes that her financial independence allows her to write "lo que me gusta, como quiero y al ritmo que me viene bien, que en mi caso es muy lento" (what I like, as I like, and at a rhythm that suits me, which in my case is very slow) (letter, 31 August 1998). An author's choice of publishing house and agent, or lack of agent, influences whether a writer is told what and how to write at a certain time. She also confesses that the destiny of several of her texts depended on the coincidental rise of particular popular trends. Her first book, *Biografías y genios, traidores, sabios y suicidas según antiguos documentos* (Biographies and Geniuses, Traitors, Wisemen, and Suicidals according to Ancient Documents) (1973), is a novel that comprises short essays influenced by Jorge Luis Borges. The book was published during the same time that Latin American boom authors appeared on the Spanish literary scene and found a welcoming audience. In a similar fashion, *El rapto del Santo Grial*

(1984) was influenced by the author's research in medieval studies and was launched when Umberto Eco's *The Name of the Rose* became a popular success. In part because of the appearance of Eco's best-selling novel and movie, *El rapto* received the attention of the Herralde Prize committee, became a finalist in 1984, and sold extremely well.

While Díaz-Mas believes that fashions may determine the destiny of one's text, she also believes that book reviews do not influence a novel's success. She claims that newspaper articles written about books in Spain function "más como publicidad del libro que como valoración de su contenido" (more as an advertisement of a book than as an evaluation of its content) (letter, 31 August 1998). She compares the articles to the way sodas are advertised: through an advertisement, we learn that the drink exists; we don't believe that the particular brand is the most refreshing one or the best-tasting one. In literature, she claims, the same occurs. Most readers do not believe what critics say, partly because their negative or positive reviews are influenced by textually extraneous events "que van desde los gustos personales del crítico, las fobias y rencillas del mundillo literario (hay críticas que se escriben en venganza por enfrentamientos personales o para halagar a un amigo) o los intereses editoriales del medio de comunicación en que se publica la crítica (hay periódicos que son propietarios también de editoras de libros y utilizan las páginas literarias del diario para hacer propaganda descarada de sus propios productos)" (that range from the personal tastes of critics, the phobias and the quarrels of the literary world [there are reviews that are written in vengeance because of personal confrontations or to flatter a friend] or the editorial interest of the medium in which the review is published [there are newspapers that are also owned by book publishers and they use the literary pages of the daily newspaper to shamelessly promote their own products]) (ibid.). Subsequently, the general public uses these critiques to find out about the existence of a new book, and it is only when an individual reads the book that he or she will evaluate its quality. According to Díaz-Mas, this theory explains why books that receive bad reviews may sell exceptionally well and why excellent books may not receive any public attention at all. Reviews serve to inform the readers; they do not reflect the quality of a text.

On the subject of books written by women, Díaz-Mas says that critics try to be either politically correct and write benevolent reviews or they push the works written by women into the "ghetto," as she calls it, of feminist literature, "lo cual es una manera de 'ningunearla', como dicen los mexicanos" (which is a manner of ignoring/denying her being, as Mexicans would say) (letter, 31 August 1998).

Rosa Montero (b. 1951 in Madrid)

While Rosa Montero is one of the most recognized and popular writers in Spain today, she admits to being conscious and, to some degree, influenced by market politics. Montero explains that when she writes a text, she does not think about the existence of readers. It is not until she is done writing that she becomes aware of her audience, because "QUIERES QUE TE LEAN, y que te lean cuantos más mejor, y en definitiva, sin ese lector al otro lado de tu escritura, tu escritura misma acabaría por morir. . . . De modo que el lector es absolutamente necesario, y el mercado es lo que regula ese contacto entre tu obra y el lector" (YOU WANT THEM TO READ YOU, and the more that they read you the better, and certainly, without that reader at the other end of your writing, your writing would end up dead. . . . For this reason, the reader is absolutely necessary, and the market is what regulates that contact between your work and the reader) (e-mail message, 22 July 1998). The problem, says Montero, is that the market contaminates the relationship between author and reader and author and text. Montero believes that the market is manipulative, loud, and omnipresent. Every writer, she says, feels the existence of the fashions and forces of the industry. The obligation of a writer is to resist these pressures and to be on guard "para no caer y no perderte" (in order not to fall and lose yourself) (ibid.).[1]

Montero explains that her sixth novel, *Bella y oscura* (Beautiful and Obscure) (1993), influenced the future of her literary production. *Bella,* written in the fantasy genre, did not receive positive reviews and was not regarded by the public as highly as Montero had expected. When Montero moved away from fantasy and wrote the realist text *La hija de Caníbal* (The Daughter of Cannibal) (1997), she was surprised to find that the novel was loudly applauded. Montero admits in hindsight that her choice of realism for the framework of the book was partly due to the rejection she had experienced from the publication of *Bella.* Curiously, she says, after the publication of *La hija* she felt more confident and free to return to the fantastic in her subsequent project.

To emphasize the influence that the market has on an author, Montero describes the experience of a friend, the Basque author Bernardo Atxaga, who wrote an unsuccessful, ninety-page novel called *Esos cielos* (Those Skies). Montero explains that "me decía el pobre, desesperado: 'Es que la gente no acepta ese formato de la novela corta. . . . No me volverá a pasar porque no volveré a escribir una novela corta semejante': ¿Te das cuenta? [dice Montero]. El exterior acaba influyéndote" (The poor guy told me, in despair, "People do not accept that format of the short novel. . . . It will not happen to me again because I will not write another similar short novel": Do you see [says Montero]? The exterior ends up influencing you) (e-mail message, 22 July 1998).

For Montero, being a writer means that one has to be a showperson. In the 1990s, writing was just one step in the publication of a book. Today, you also need to appear on television and radio, in photographs, posters, and book jackets. These extraneous tasks add enormously to the work of writers who have to run from one place to another "haciendo el idota" (acting like an idiot). This circus has been taken to an extreme by authors such as Etxebarría, about whose activities Montero says: "hay gente que está dispuesta a casi todo para promocionarse. Terminaremos todos convertidos en payasos" (there are people who are prepared to do almost anything to promote themselves. We will all end up turned into clowns) (e-mail message, 22 July 1998).

Clara Obligado (b. 1950 in Argentina)

Clara Obligado has clearly formulated and expressed the connection between her work, her position in the market, and the manner in which the industry affects the visibility of her production. Obligado has published two novels; the first, *La hija de Marx* (Marx's Daughter), received the Premio Femenino Lumen in 1996 and the second, *Si un hombre vivo te hace llorar* (If a Live Man Makes You Cry), was published by Planeta in 1998. *La hija* is an erotic, historical, and feminist novel in the form of a biography. It is a text that breaks many taboos as it includes scenes of incest, homosexuality, and child sexuality. Obligado explains that this text was rejected by ten publishing houses, all of which justified their rejections in long explicative letters. It was as if, she says, the book created discomfort because "yo trabajaba una especie de intergénero entre la novela histórica y la erótica, entre el realismo puro y duro y la novela moderna. No apostaba en absoluto por el amor, cuestionaba el lugar de ciertos pro-hombres de la izquierda, en fin, temas que yo trabajé con bastante ingenuidad y que luego resultaron mucho más molestos de lo que yo misma podía esperar" (I worked a kind of intergenre between the historical novel and the erotic, between pure and hard realism and the modern novel. I absolutely did not bet on love; I questioned the position of certain pro-men from the left—in short, topics that I used with a certain amount of ingenuity and that later ended up being much more bothersome than I could have expected) (letter, 25 June 1998). She initially did not find a publisher for *La hija* because the text could not be comfortably inserted into any existing collection.

The limited amount of space in bookstores and catalogs determined the second step of the publication of *La hija* as well. The novel appeared in print media at the same time as two other texts from the same collection. Obligado explains that on a Thursday her novel was to appear in newspapers, while on a Wednesday and a Friday two other novels, by known writers, were to be reviewed as well. When the books were presented to the press, "¿a cuáles piensas tú que le [hicieron] la crítica? A las tres es imposible, no hay espacio. ¿Cuáles [fueron] colocadas en el escaparate de las librerías?" (which ones do you think were reviewed? To review all three is impossible; there is no space. Which ones were placed in store windows?) (letter, 25 June 1998). Obligado found that the limited amount of media space, and her access to it, became a determining factor in the visibility of her book.

In a letter to Obligado in 1998, I told her of an episode that emphasizes the agency of an author in manipulating the forces of the market. After presenting a paper at a United States university in which I discussed some of the same issues as covered in this book, one scholar asked me: "Do you mean to tell me that an author's career may fall into ruin because of a football game?" In response to this question, Obligado told me the following story concerning the presentation of one of her books:

> Resulta que en Madrid, a partir de mayo, no se puede hacer nada de jueves a domingo, porque todos los días transmiten partidos [de fútbol]. Elegí, pues, un poco en plan provocación, otro poco porque simplemente me daba la gana, ese día tan señalado [del día de la Copa Mundial].
>
> Mis amigos me dijeron que era suicida, que no vendría ni dios. Los de la editorial confiaban en que seríamos más o menos tres en la sala. El discurso de la presentadora, Lourdes Ortiz, una escritora muy interesante, también estaba preparado en ese sentido. Prensa, por supuesto que no había. Pero público sí. Cerca de cuatrocientas personas. . . .
>
> Pero al día siguiente salió en los periódicos como rareza absoluta, y me llamaron de varios programas ¡deportivos! para que comentara cómo se me había ocurrido la idea. Todavía hoy me dicen ¿tú eres la que se atrevió a presentar un libro el día de la Copa? . . .
>
> En fin, la anécdota tiene su gracia. (letter, 8 April 1998)

[It turns out that in Madrid, from May on, one cannot do anything from Thursday to Sunday, because football games are on television on a daily basis. I chose, then, partly to provoke and partly because I simply felt like it, this notable day (of the World Cup).

My friends told me that it was suicide and that not even God would come. People from the publishing house were sure that we would be about three in the room. The address presented by Lourdes Ortiz, a very interesting writer, was also prepared based on this assumption. Press, of course, was not there. But there was an audience. Close to four hundred people. . . .

But the next day, like an absolute oddity, it appeared in newspapers, and several sports programs called me and asked me to comment on how I came up with the idea! Even today, people say to me: are you the one who dared to present a book on the day of the Cup? . . .

Anyway, the anecdote is humorous.]

While an author can have a certain amount of agency in determining the plight of his or her future, Obligado believes that most books are born with a predetermined destiny. Before books arrive in stores, publishing houses already know (with a slight margin of error) whether they will sell. If the publishing house invests in promotional material, if the writer works as a journalist for an important newspaper, or if he or she is a television personality, the text will sell well, independent of its literary quality: "En este sentido la ley del mercado parecería ser: Sé primero famoso, y luego escritor" (In this sense the law of the market seems to be "Be famous first and then become a writer") (letter, 25 June 1998). Nevertheless, Obligado has also shown that when authors are aware of industry workings, they can play with market coordinates and try to shift them to their advantage.

Marta Sanz (b. 1967 in Madrid)

Marta Sanz is a professor of Hispanic literature at the Universidad Antonio de Nebrija in Madrid and the author of several short stories and two novels, including *El frío* (The Cold) (1995), *Lenguas muertas* (Dead Languages) (1997), and *Los mejores tiempos* (The Best of Times) (2001). Sanz finds solace in a publishing house, Destino, where she can count on the good advice of the director Andreu Teixidor de Ventós. She has never used an agent, and she signs contracts with Destino after she submits each text (many authors today sign contracts for books that have not yet been written and must meet certain technical and thematic criteria, or they sign contracts for three books at a time). Sanz explains that once her novel is complete, she hands it over to the editor who distributes the book to the media and the most important critics in the country. She claims, directly in contradiction with Paloma Díaz-Mas, that "en manos de estos últimos, queda la decisión de que tu obra aparezca, se conozca y se valore o sea condenada a la más absoluta de las invisibilidades" (in the hands of the latter lies the decision as to whether your work will appear, will become known, and will be valued or condemned to the most absolute of invisibilities) (e-mail message, 28 Aug. 1999).

Sanz's texts have sold well, partly because they have been reviewed in literary supplements such as *El País* and *ABC*, and partly because critics have categorized her as "Una escritora minoritaria de la que se esperan cosas, precisamente porque aún no [ha] entrado en esos monstruosos canales de difusión que desdibujan los límites tradicionales entre el best seller y la literatura de calidad" (A minority writer of whom things can be expected, precisely because [she has] not yet entered in those monstrous channels of diffusion that blur the traditional limits between the best seller and literature of quality) (e-mail message, 28 Aug. 1999).

Sanz believes that she will not burn out as quickly as other authors who depend on their work for their livelihood. This situation, she says, is her greatest paradox: "no poder vivir de hacer lo que más te gusta y saber que ese inconveniente existencial redunda positivamente en tus labores creativas" (not to be able to live from what I like to do most, and to know that this existential inconvenience echoes positively in my creative labors) (e-mail message, 28 Aug. 1999). Sanz believes that she has the room to forget about the pressures of the market and the taste of readers and to adventure into creatively more diverse areas that are less conditioned by the commercial canon. She says: "Para mí esa posibilidad es bastante positiva porque los planteamientos que vinculan la calidad literaria con el nivel de ventas me parecen demagógicos y, además, creo que contradicen las relaciones entre el mercado y creación de los grandes hitos de la historia de la literatura y del arte" (For me, this possibility is quite positive because I find the approaches that tie the literary quality to the level of sales demagogical, and, anyway, I think that they contradict the relationship between the market and the creation of the great landmarks of the history of literature and art) (ibid.). She believes that the accessibility and entertainment level of contemporary works has erased literature's reflexive, critical, and interrogative qualities. Literature today, she says, has been minimized to a mere "laxante" (laxative) that helps readers escape their daily routines. Sanz is conscious that every author desires to communicate his or her reality in the most effective manner possible. She also tries to reach this audience, but without giving up her fundamental beliefs in the quality of her work.

Lola Beccaria (b. 1963 in El Ferrol, Galicia)

Lola Beccaria has written *La debutante* (The Debutante) (1996) and *La luna de Jorge* (Jorge's Moon), finalist of the 2001 Nadal Prize. She believes that the world of publishing has traditionally belonged to men: "Eran hombres los que editaban, los que escogían las obras que se publicaban, los que hacían las críticas, los que llevaban los suplementos culturales de los periódicos, y las revistas culturales y literarias. Por todo ello, se editaban obras que respondieran al gusto de los hombres, a sus preocupaciones e intereses" (It was men who edited, who chose the works that were to be published, who wrote the critiques, who were in charge of the cultural supplements of the newspapers, and the cultural and literary magazines. Because of all this, works were published that coincided with the taste of men, with their preoccupations and interests) (e-mail message, 30 July 1999).[2] Women, she says have slowly introduced themselves into the publishing industry, especially as agents, and have changed the market to include the taste of women. Many publishers, says Beccaria, have realized that works written by women connect especially well with a certain group of readers. Thanks to this, authors such as Almudena Grandes and Lucía Etxebarría have become commercial successes. Nevertheless, Beccaria believes that male publishers are still not taking enough risks when it comes to the publication of texts written by women: "Vamos camino de ello, pero aún queda un largo recorrido" (We are on our way, but we still have a long way to go) (ibid.).

Paula Izquierdo (b. 1962 in Madrid)

Paula Izquierdo has published two novels, *La vida sin secreto* (Secretless Life) (1997) and *El hueco de tu cuerpo* (The Cavity of Your Body) (2000). Izquierdo has found that her work is often reduced to her physical appearance. Because of her good looks, Izquierdo has to carefully choose the interviews and the media appearances so as not to reduce her and her work to sexualized objects. Two experiences in particular have made her tread cautiously in her relations with the mass media. The first one was an interview that was conducted with *Elle* magazine. Izquierdo is one of four female personalities who appeared in the May 2000 issue of the magazine. The cover shows a female buttock and the headline, "Especial culo: 4 famosas nos dan la espalda y descubren su otra cara" (Butt Special: 4 Famous Women Turn Their Backs to Us and Uncover Their Other Face). In one photograph, Izquierdo is dressed in pink, exposing her seminude back, and holding up her long dark hair in a seductive pose. On one side, the copy reads: "Nunca me miro por detrás. Me basta con gustarme de frente, que es lo que yo veo" (I never look at myself from behind. I am satisfied with liking myself from the front, which is what I see), and in a box, in small letters, the readers are challenged to identify the woman who "Ha pasado diez años de su vida bailando sobre los escenarios. Pero cambió los tutús por un doctorado en psicología. Ahora nos sorprende con su segunda novela. ¿Adivinas?" (She has spent ten years of her life dancing on stage. But she turned in the tutus for a doctorate in psychology. Now she surprises us with her second novel. Can you guess?) (52). When the viewers turn to page 54, they are confronted with a Paula Izquierdo, whose face is half-covered by her flowing dark hair and whose blue eyes piercingly look at the readers. Her photograph is surrounded by a short interview in which one of Izquierdo's comments is highlighted: "El culo es sexy. Pero a veces lo es más enseñar el ombligo" (The butt is sexy. But sometimes it is even more sexy to show the navel). When this issue of *Elle* arrived on Izquierdo's doorstep, she says that she was devastated to see that what she thought was going to be a thoughtful discussion of the image of women's bodies—a topic that the author deals with in her second novel—was instead a sexist exposition of body parts that once again emphasized Izquierdo's marketing as a hot, sexy, "chica mona" (cute girl).

On another occasion, a television station approached Izquierdo to do an interview concerning *El hueco*. She accepted with enthusiasm since a television appearance can increase a book's sales figures multifold. On the day that the filming was to take place, the female director asked Izquierdo to read the first few sentences of her novel: "Sus ojos se pasean perdidos, peregrinan por el techo que no es suyo. Retira las sábanas con cuidado, se incorpora lentamente en la cama, desnuda, girándose hasta alcanzar el borde del colchón" (Lost, her eyes wander, they migrate along the wall that is not hers. She carefully pulls back the sheets, she slowly sits up in bed, naked, turning until she reaches the end of the mattress) (11). She was also asked to impersonate the protagonist who, as the above quotation suggests, is getting out of bed naked. Disgusted, Izquierdo rejected acting the scene and left the set. At that moment, she said good-bye to the possibilities of appearing on best-seller lists, making higher claims to fame, signing contracts with better publishers, and receiving a higher salary.

Izquierdo explains that her looks have hurt her path to becoming a serious writer. Many female authors, she says, are asked to partake in the outrageous tactics that have made Etxebarría famous: "If Lucía will expose it all, why won't you?" she is often asked. Some people, she claims, think that her looks are to credit for her publications, yet the people who make these assumptions have not read her work. Izquierdo believes that while male writers can appear in an Armani suit without receiving as much as a comment, female authors who dress well or expose any part of their bodies are immediately objectified. Izquierdo believes that this phenomenon occurs because it reduces the space that women authors occupy on a professional level and therefore decreases the threat to their male counterparts.

In order to counterattack her "chica mona" image, Izquierdo has begun to write a series of weekly pieces called "Escritores europeos ante el milenio" (European Writers Confront the Millennium), in which she introduces and discusses the work of different authors. These pieces appear in *El Cultural* (in print and on the Internet). By recreating her image as that of an intellectual writer, she hopes to thoroughly confuse her reading audience and redirect her career (interview, 11 July 2000).

Care Santos (b. 1970 in Barcelona)

Care Santos is the founder of the Asociación de Jóvenes Escritores (Association of Young Writers), which helps young authors deal with the demands and politics of the literary market. The group began in 1992 (and ended in 1999) with fifteen members and grew, in just over a year, to five hundred writers. Santos is the author of several short stories, books of poetry, and novels for adolescent and adult audiences. Her first adult novel, *El tango del perdedor* (The Tango of the Loser) (1997), taught her the meaning of commercial contamination. She wrote this book with the desire to please and chose a voice that would reach all types of readers, a voice without great stylistic or formal pretensions. What happened? She asks: "Que fue a mí a quien no gustó la novela, y eso es malísimo. No reniego de ella, pero cuando la releo pienso que no debería haberme preocupado por factores extraliterarios, ni haber corrido tanto. Ahí aprendí la lección: nunca más voy a escribir para otros, sólo para mí. Y voy a tratar de hacer algo que me vea con ánimos de defender" (It was me who did not like the novel, and that is really bad. I do not renounce it, but when I reread it I think that I should not have preoccupied myself with extraliterary factors, nor should I have hurried so much. There I learned the lesson: never again will I write for others, only for myself. And I am going to try to do something that I will feel good about defending) (e-mail message, 15 June 1999). Santos is aware of the need to promote her texts and herself as much as possible: "La publicidad es fundamental, y aunque las campañas de promoción siempre resultan pesadas para los autores, sabemos que de ellas depende el éxito del libro" (Advertising is fundamental, and even though promotional campaigns are always a pain for the authors, we know that the success of a book depends on them) (ibid.). Santos admits that even though she attempts to conserve literary purity, she is not immune to contamination. We all live in the market, she explains, in some way or another. We are all influenced by what is published, what is liked, and what is sold, even if we do not buy it or like it. The market forms part of our reality and the rules of the game in which we participate.

Santos's publisher was Alba, a house that belongs to Prensa Ibérica, a company that owns newspapers in many Spanish provinces. For her first novel, Santos was interviewed by a friend, Tino Pertierra, and photos of her were taken by Eduardo Rius, her former husband. She was also interviewed by several local radio stations and, because of a personal contract, Radio Nacional de España. The presentation of *El tango* took place in Barcelona, where the actress Amparo Moreno read a section of her book and a journalist friend, Carlos Herrera, "habló maravillas. Escuchándole parecía que hubiera escrito un libro interesante y todo" (spoke highly. Listening to him it seemed as though I had even written an interesting book) (e-mail message, 15 June 1999). Nevertheless, Alba ran only one thousand copies of the novel—"una miseria" (a misery). They placed one advertisement for the book that erroneously appeared in the economy section of a Barcelona newspaper, there were no television interviews, and Santos was not asked to sign books or take part in the Feria del Libro. The promotion of her book amounted to practically nothing, and, years later, Santos realized that this lack of promotion contributed to many readers and critics being unaware of the existence of her text.

Her second novel, *Trigal con cuervos* (Wheat Field with Crows) (1999), had a different fate. For this novel, she was honored with the Ateneo de Sevilla Prize, and subsequently experienced a large amount of advertising and promotion. She had to travel to many different cities. Her book was reviewed in national, local, and specialized papers and magazines, and she took part in a large number of interviews. Looking back at her grand tour, Santos jokingly explains her new hypothesis: prize committees choose young authors because writers today need to have the physical stamina and endurance to go through the intensity of today's promotional campaigns.

Espido Freire (b. 1974 in Bilbao)

Espido Freire is one of the youngest writers to receive the Planeta Prize, which she won in 1999 for *Melocotones helados* (Frozen Peaches). That year was also the first time that the winner and the finalist of the Planeta were both women. According to Freire, this supposed special pressure by the media and more attention on behalf of certain publications. Once Freire received the prize, she participated in book presentations throughout Spain that took several weeks and covered cities such as Madrid, La Coruña, Bilbao, Zaragoza, Barcelona, Santander, Valencia, Seville, Málaga, Vitoria, and Bilbao. In these cities, she gave press conferences and signed books in commercial centers such as the department store El Corte Inglés. She also traveled to Mexico, Venezuela, Colombia, and Argentina, where she took part in book presentations, receptions at embassies, book-signing events, and up to sixteen interviews a day. The campaign was carefully planned by the publishing house and covered all terrain: from television to print and radio advertising, and from specialized to general information sources. The promotion was ethical, she says, and effective.

Freire explains that the image that was created of her in the media was one that was concocted by each individual journalist, not by the publishing house. From the very beginning, Freire was conscious of the "críticas que concita este premio y de mi excesiva visibilidad, pero en ocasiones los errores biográficos o las opiniones de los medios han dado lugar a artículos en los que se me consideraba frívola y coqueta" (reviews that this prize incites and of my excessive visibility. But on occasion, the biographical errors or the opinion of the media has produced articles in which I was considered frivolous and coquettish) (e-mail message, 4 Sept. 2000). In contrast, the image that the author has always tried to maintain is that of a serious, professional, and discreet person.

With the Planeta Prize comes a certain amount of built-in visibility. The promotion in which Freire willingly took part allowed the book to reach its thirteenth edition in less than a year. Freire admits that the large number of copies sold would not have been possible without the campaign. On the other hand, she explains, she had already been collaborating with various media and she continued to do so throughout 1999, in order to establish a certain popularity with the media.

Freire considers herself a mere vehicle of communication in the commercial campaign that has made her so famous. She believes that her literary production has been affected neither by her popularity nor by her constant travels: "Había contado ya con ello, y no era tan inocente como para no saber qué me esperaba al presentarme al Planeta, de modo que ya había preparado otras obras, que aparecerán a lo largo del próximo año, sin que el ajetreo de la promoción influyera" (I had already counted on it and I was not so innocent as to not know what awaited me when I was presented the Planeta, for which reason I had already prepared other works that will appear throughout the next year, without having the bustle of the promotion influence me) (e-mail message, 4 Sept. 2000).

In reference to being a woman, Freire believes that while she has not felt any discrimination from other writers and colleagues, the mass media "ha dejado, en ocasiones, algo que desear. Paternalismo, actitudes condescendientes y una atención excesiva a mi aspecto físico y a mi *look* han sido constantes" (has left, at times, much to be desired. Paternalism, condescending attitudes, and an excessive atention to my physical appearance and my look have been constants) (e-mail message, 4 Sept. 2000). Regarding the comparison of Freire with Etxebarría, she explains: "Pocas polémicas en torno a mí y a mi premio me han resultado tan desagradables como el intento de enfrentarnos a Lucía Etxebarría y a mí" (Few polemics concerning me and my prize have been quite as unpleasant as the attempt to confront Lucía Etxebarría and myself) (e-mail message, 7 Sept. 2000). Freire explains that she and Etxebarría have nothing in common: they are not of the same age, character, background, or literary trajectory. They have not won the same prize, they don't publish with the same houses, they don't have the same literary or lifestyle philosophies. What the two authors do share is a deep love for literature and a respect for each other.

Freire does not censure nor approve of the methods that Etxebarría uses to confront her audience and the media. For Freire, Etxebarría is an author of much success who has had to deal with a large number of extraliterary critiques. Freire does what she considers best for her own career: "Tiendo a no preocuparme demasiado por lo que los demás opinen. Si eso complace en mayor o menor medida a determinados sectores, no es mi problema" (I tend to not worry too much about the opinion of others. Whether this pleases to a greater or lesser degree certain sectors is not my problem) (ibid.). Freire believes that she is so often compared to Etxebarría because only a few years ago, Etxebarría was the only young female author who had received such a prestigious literary prize and had been inundated with such a large amount of media attention. At the heart of the issue, says Freire, lies the ignorance of an establishment that does not recognize any other but the most celebrated and visible women writers.

Notes

1. I use this quote in the introduction and here to emphasize Montero's message in this more personal realm.

2. I use this quote in the introduction and here to emphasize Beccaria's message in this more personal realm.

Conclusion

Each text in this study uses the body as its instrument of subversion as well as its selling point. The (erotic) female body becomes the center of all six novels, and the body plays with the desire of characters and readers alike. The female body—as a reflection of its real-life relation to the discriminatory and sexist practices of the industry—becomes the site at which the limits and powers of its construction are discussed and at which meaning is established and can be altered. The novels studied in this book bridge an approach to marketing and visual culture so as to contribute to an understanding of the role of the mass media in the creation of contemporary Spanish women's texts. The six chapters point to the visual field of signification within which the female author has the power to determine the image that she can construct on either a fictional or a real level.

El sueño de Venecia by Paloma Díaz-Mas redefines the concept of feminine literature by deauthorizing the narrative voice through visual systems of signification. Through five chapters connected by a painting, the meaning of which shifts in each chapter, *El sueño* exposes the manners in which female bodies are visually constructed and bodies of writing are interpreted. The novel is the foreground for an era in which the visual and the textual collide in order to produce a new work—a newly identified body of narrative.

Urraca by Lourdes Ortiz places the body of the protagonist at the center of the text's attention through the mechanism of the cut, in order to point to woman's visual power to subvert historical authority. Ortiz applies one of the mechanisms with which the world of promotion has attracted its audiences for years—the cut—and she takes recourse to one of the most powerful stimuli of the marketing industry—erotic seduction. In Ortiz's novel, the narrator emphasizes the cuts by which the female voice has been excised from historical accounts and truthful representations. More than as a sexual entity, Urraca's body serves as a metanarrative device that is used to increase the pleasure of the text and to unsettle the historically fixed identity of the female through subtle promotional mechanisms.

Solitario de amor by Cristina Peri Rossi undermines the act of fixation and redelineates the erotic female body in terms of the same system that constructs it. The novel exposes a process of fetishization through the limited perspective of a male narrator who tries to capture his ex-lover's body through writing. Because of the sexual and existential effects that the body has on the narrator, the female figure becomes the site of a discussion of linguistic powers and limits. The text re-presents the female body in order to fixate on it as the ever existing second skin of the protagonist. But as language fails to reproduce fully the narrator's object of desire, he decides to turn himself into a product in order to break down the barriers of distance and absence. He attempts to cover his lover like a piece of clothing but fails because the female body does not allow itself to be held down. The novel points to the erotic performance of the female body as a site of resistance.

El amor es un juego solitario by Esther Tusquets demonstrates that even when the female body is literally and even violently subdued, it can undermine the submissiveness of its position by pointing to the uniqueness of the visual system within which the protagonist constructs her identity. *El amor* opens up the representation of the female body to the system within which it is translated. The analysis of the three characters of the novel through focalization points to advertising's inclusion of both male and female viewers in the commodifying process. The fluidity of viewing positions rejects polar associations and shows how the female body, even when it seems to lose its narrative and physical authority, may keep the upper hand.

Las edades de Lulú by Almudena Grandes makes the consumers' eyewitness position explicit and actively involves them in the repositioning of the female body. Grandes's novel incites readers' awareness of the role of the female body (as author and as character) in the process of creating meaning. *Las edades* foregrounds the validity of the art of women writers who appropriate the female body on an erotic level and on a level that questions the value of their own subjectivity and position in relation to the dominant forms of writing and promotion.

Lucía Etxebarría, the youngest member of this group, turns her own body into an advertisement in order to subvert the representation of female authors in the media. She takes the system into her own hands and appropriates the industry's power of promotion to increase the number of readers of her feminist messages. Etxebarría uses the power of visual marketing to uncover the forces involved in the making of contemporary (female) writers and to open new spaces for future texts by female authors.

Contemporary Spanish Women's Narrative and the Publishing Industry examines the factors that contribute to the dissemination, positioning, and reception of the work by Spanish women writers at the end of the millennium. Instead of bringing these factors out from their textual referents, women writers speak for themselves and describe the formation of their own bodies (of narrative) in the public eye. As the critical eye of this study teases out the authority of the textual female body, it finds itself uncovering the female body of the author. As she stands before literary critics, having shared her personal experiences in the book market, they are left having to redress approaches to the study of literature written by women. With a body that is in the process of rejecting its biologically determined characteristics—"literatura feminina"—and a narrative that is redefining itself in the eyes of its public, it may be time to approach the study of literature written by Spanish female authors in the twenty-first century from a new angle.

Works Cited

Alcalá, Ángel. *Inquisición española y mentalidad inquisitorial.* Barcelona: Ariel, 1984.

Alfieri, Carlos. "Entrevista con Fernando R. Lafuente." *Cuadernos Hispanoamericanos* 564 (June 1997): 7–17.

"Almudena Grandes: 'El erotismo es ideal para contar historias.'" *Antena Semanal,* 1 Apr. 1990, 16–18.

"Ángeles de Irisarri saca partido a las mujeres de la Historia de España." *El Mundo,* 7 Oct. 1999, <http://www.elmundoliterario.es>.

Antolín Cochrane, Helena. "Androgynous Voices in the Novels of Cristina Peri Rossi." *Mosaic* 30.3 (1997): 97–114.

Apter, Emily, and William Pietz, eds. *Fetishism As Cultural Discourse.* Ithaca: Cornell University Press, 1993.

Arnaiz, Joaquín. "Lucía Etxebarría: 'No hay chicas malas y chicas buenas.'" *El Mundo,* 24 Apr. 1999, 63.

Arteaga del Alcázar, Almudena de. *La princesa de Éboli.* Barcelona: Ediciones Martínez Roca, 1998.

Ballarín, Rosa. "Lucía Etxebarría: Calma aparente." *Quimera* 5.55 (25–28).

Balsamo, Anne. *Technologies of the Gendered Body: Reading Cyborg Women.* Durham: Duke University Press, 1996.

"Barómetro de hábitos de compra y lectura de libros: primer trimester 2001." Ministerio de Educación, Cultura, y Deporte. <http://www.federacioneditores.org/noticias /FG_LisaNoticias.es>.

Barthes, Roland. *The Pleasure of the Text.* Trans. Richard Miller. New York: Hill and Wang, 1975.

Basanta, Ángel. "Beatriz y los cuerpos celestes." *ABC literario,* 13 Feb. 1998, 13.

Baudrillard, Jean. "The Precession of Simulacra." In *Media and Cultural Studies: Key-Works.* Ed. Meenakshi Gigi Durham and Douglas M. Kellner. Malden, Mass.: Blackwell, 2001. 521–49.

———. *Seduction.* Trans. Brian Singer. New York: St. Martin's Press, 1979.

Works Cited

Belch, George, and Michael Belch. *Introduction to Advertising and Promotion Management.* Boston: Irwin, 1990.

Bellver, Catherine. "The Language of Eroticism in the Novels of Esther Tusquets." *Anales de la Literatura Española Contemporánea* 9.1–3 (1984): 13–27.

Bengoa, María. "Las descaradas chicas de Etxebarría." *El Correo Español,* 21 Apr. 1999, 56.

Benjamin, Walter. "The Work of Art in the Age of Mechanical Reproduction." In *Illuminations.* Trans. Harry Zohn. New York: Harcourt, 1968. 217–51.

Berger, John. *Ways of Seeing.* London: Penguin, 1972.

Botana, Alicia V. "'El sexo se aprende, no es una cuestión de medidas.'" *Dunia,* Feb. 1998, 56–59.

Bourdieu, Pierre. *The Field of Cultural Production: Essays on Art and Literature.* Ed. Randal Johnson. New York: Columbia University Press, 1993.

Bretz, Mary Lee. *Concha Espina.* Boston: Twayne, 1980.

Brooks, Peter. *Body Work: Objects of Desire in Modern Narrative.* Cambridge, Mass.: Harvard University Press, 1993.

Brown, Jonathan. *Velázquez: Painter and Courtier.* New Haven: Yale University Press, 1986.

Brown, Lesley, ed. *The New Shorter Oxford English Dictionary on Historical Principles.* Oxford: Clarendon Press, 1993.

Carbayo Abengózar, Mercedes. *Buscando un lugar entre mujeres: Buceo en la España de Carmen Martín Gaite.* Málaga: Universidad de Málaga, 1998.

Carlson, Marvin. *Performance: A Critical Introduction.* New York: Routledge, 1996.

Caso, Ángeles. "La crítica sigue perdonando la vida a las escritoras." *El Mundo,* 29 Nov. 2001, <http://www.elmundolibro.es>.

Castilla, C., and A. F. Rubio. "Los ejecutivos ponen contra las cuerdas a los autores." *El País,* 23 Apr. 1995, 31.

Ciplijauskaité, Biruté. "Lyric Memory, Oral History, and Its Shaping of Self in Spanish Narrative." *Forum for Modern Language Studies* 28.4 (1992): 390–400.

———. *La mujer insatisfecha: El adulterio en la novela realista.* Barcelona: Edhasa, 1984.

Coupland, Douglas. *Generation X: Tales for an Accelerated Culture.* New York: St. Martin's Press, 1991.

Davies, Catherine. *Spanish Women's Writing, 1849–1996.* London: Anthlone Press, 1998.

Díaz, Janet. *Ana María Matute.* New York: Twayne, 1971.

Díaz-Mas, Paloma. *El sueño de Venecia.* Barcelona: Anagrama, 1992.

Dolgin, Stacey L. "Conversación con Esther Tusquets: 'Para salir de tanta miseria.'" *Anales de la Literatura Española Contemporánea* 13.3 (1988): 397–406.

Echevarría, Ignacio. "Otra vez *Nada*." *El País Babelia,* 21 Feb. 1998, 11.

Etxebarría, Lucía. *Amor, curiosidad, prozac y dudas.* Barcelona: Plaza and Janés, 1997.

———. *Beatriz y los cuerpos celestes.* Barcelona: Destino, 1998.

———. *La Eva futura.* Barcelona: Destino, 2000.

———. *La letra futura.* Barcelona: Destino, 2000.

———. *Nosotras que no somos como las demás.* Barcelona: Destino, 1999.

Works Cited

Felman, Shoshana. *Literature and Psychoanalysis: The Question of Reading Otherwise.* Baltimore: Johns Hopkins University Press, 1982.

Ferrán, Ofelia. "La escritura y la historia: Entrevista con Paloma Díaz-Mas." *Anales de la Literatura Española Contemporánea* 22.2 (1997): 327–45.

Ferrer, Isabel. "Lulú seduce al holandés." *El País,* 11 Dec. 1990, 35.

Focillon, Henri. *The Life of Forms in Art.* New York: Zone Books, 1992.

Forster, Kurt W. "The Hamburg-America Line; or, Warburg's 'Cultural Studies between Two Continents.'" Ms. 1996.

Fraile, María José. "Entrevista a Lucía Etxebarría." *Mujeractual,* 28 Nov. 2001, <http://www.mujeractual.com/entrevistas/etxebarría/index.html>.

Freixas, Laura. *Literatura y mujeres.* Barcelona: Destino, 2000.

———. "'Lo femenino' en la crítica literaria española." *Letra Internacional* 73 (2001): 41–49.

———. *Madres e hijas.* Barcelona: Anagrama, 1996.

Freud, Sigmund. "Fetishism." *Standard Edition of the Complete Psychological Works of Sigmund Freud.* Ed. James Strachey. New York: Institute of Psycho-Analysis and Hogarth Press, 1961. 149–57.

Freud, Sigmund. *Minutes from the Vienna Psychoanalytical Society: III. 1910–1911.* Trans. Herman Nunberg and Ernst Federn. New York: International Universities Press, 1974.

———. *Three Essays on the Theory of Sexuality.* Trans. and ed. James Strachey. New York: Basic Books, 1962.

Fuss, Diana. "Fashion and the Homospectatorial Look." *Critical Inquiry* 18 (Summer 1992): 713–37.

Gamman, Lorraine, and Merja Makinen. *Female Fetishism: A New Look.* London: Lawrence and Wishart, 1994.

Gazarian Gautier, Marie-Lise, ed. "Carmen Laforet." *Interviews with Spanish Writers.* Elmwood Park, Ill.: Dalkey Archive Press, 1991. 151–64.

Geisdorfer Feal, Rosemary. "Cristina Peri Rossi and the Erotic Imagination." In *Reinterpreting the Spanish American Essay: Women Writers of the Nineteenth and Twentieth Centuries.* Austin: University of Texas Press, 1995. 215–26.

Glenn, Kathleen M. "Reading and Rewriting *El sueño de Venecia.*" *Romance Languages Annual* 7 (1995): 483–90.

Gofman, Erving. *Gender Advertisements.* New York: Harper Torchbooks, 1987.

Gossy, Mary S. "Not So Lonely: A Butch-Femme Reading of Cristina Peri Rossi's *Solitario de amor.*" In *Bodies and Biases: Sexualities in Hispanic Culture and Literature.* Ed. David William Foster and Roberto Reis. Minneapolis: University of Minnesota Press, 1991. 238–45.

Graham, Helen, and Jo Labanyi, eds. *Spanish Cultural Studies: An Introduction.* Oxford: Oxford University Press, 1995.

Grandes, Almudena. "La conquista de una mirada." *Letra Internacional* 73 (2001): 52–62.

———. *Las edades de Lulú.* Barcelona: Tusquets, 1989.

Haraway, Donna. "The Persistence of Vision." In *Writing on the Body: Female Embodiment and Feminist Theory.* Ed. Katie Conboy, Nadia Medina, and Sarah Stanbury. New York: Columbia University Press, 1997. 283–95.

Hart, Stephen. "Esther Tusquets: Sex, Excess, and the Dangerous Supplement of Language." *Antípodas* 3 (July 1991): 85–98.

Hernández, Juana Amelia. "La postmodernidad en la ficción de Paloma Díaz-Mas." *Romance Languages Annual* 2 (1990): 450–54.

Herrera, Ángel-Antonio. "Almudena Grandes: El sexo de los libros." *Man,* Feb. 1990, 56–58.

Hutcheon, Linda. *Narcissistic Narrative: The Metafictional Paradox.* Waterloo, Ont.: Wilfrid Laurier University Press, 1980.

Informe SGAE, sobre hábitos de consumo cultural. Madrid: Sociedad General de Autores de España, 2000.

Irisarri, Ángeles de. *La reina Urraca.* Madrid: Temas de Hoy, 2001.

Izquierdo, Paula. *El hueco de tu cuerpo.* Barcelona: Anagrama, 2000.

———. *La vida sin secreto.* Barcelona: Plaza and Janés, 1997.

Johnson, Carrol B. "La española inglesa and the Practice of Literary Production." *Viator* 19 (1988): 377–416.

Johnson, Roberta. *Carmen Laforet.* Boston: Twayne, 1981.

———. "Narrative in Culture, 1868–1936." In *The Cambridge Companion to Modern Spanish Culture.* Ed. David T. Gies. Cambridge: Cambridge University Press, 1999. 123–33.

Kahmen, Volker. *Erotic Art Today.* Trans. Peter Newmark. Greenwich, Conn.: New York Graphic Society, 1972.

Kantaris, Elia. "The Politics of Desire: Alienation and Identity in the Work of Marta Traba and Cristina Peri Rossi." *Forum for Modern Language Studies* 25.3 (1989): 248–64.

Kirkpatrick, Susan. *Las Románticas: Women Writers and Subjectivity in Spain, 1835–1850.* Berkeley: University of California Press, 1989.

"La industria editorial creació un 2.7% el año pasado y movió 270.00 millones." *El País,* 6 Sept. 2000, 37.

Langa Pizarro, M. Mar. *Del franquismo a la posmodernidad: La novela española, 1975–1999.* Murcia: Universidad de Alicante, 2000.

Laplanche, Jean, and J. B. Pontalis. *The Language of Psycho-analysis.* Trans. Donald Nicholson-Smith. New York: Norton, 1973.

Lector, Aníbal. "Ha nacido una estrella." *Qué Leer,* Feb. 1989, 25.

Levine, Linda Gould. "The Female Body As Palimpsest in the Works of Carmen Gómez-Ojea, Paloma Díaz-Mas, Ana Rosetti." *Indiana Journal of Hispanic Literatures* 2.1 (1993): 181–206.

———. "Reading, Rereading, Misreading, and Rewriting the Male Canon: The Narrative Web of Esther Tusquets's Trilogy." *Anales de la Literatura Española Contemporánea* 12.1–2 (1987): 203–17.

López de Faro, Renée. "Visto y no visto." *El País,* 28 Feb. 1993, 64–69.

Mántaras Loedel, Graciela. "La obra de Cristina Peri Rossi en la literatura erótica uruguaya." In *Cristina Peri Rossi, papeles críticos.* Ed. Rómulo Cosse et al. Montevideo: Linardi y Risso, 1995. 31–45.

Martín, Sabas. "Narrativa española tercer milenio." *Páginas Amarillas.* Madrid: Lengua de Trapo, 1997. ix–xxx.

Martín Gaite, Carmen. *Desde la ventana.* Madrid: Espasa-Calpe, 1987.

Masolver Ródenas, Juan Antonio. "Entre Madrid y Edimburgo." *La Vanguardia,* 13 Feb. 1998, 35.

McGovern, Lynn. "History and Metafiction in Lourdes Ortiz's *Urraca.*" *Cincinnati Romance Review* 13 (1994): 197–205.

———. "Lourdes Ortiz: Novela, prensa, política, etcétera." *Ojáncano,* Oct. 1994, 46–57.

Mirzoeff, Nicholas, ed. *The Visual Culture Reader.* New York: Routledge, 1998.

Mitchell, W. J. T. *Picture Theory.* Chicago: University of Chicago Press, 1994.

———. *The Reconfigured Eye: Visual Truth in the Post-Photographic Era.* Cambridge: MIT Press, 1994.

Moi, Toril. *Sexual/Textual Politics.* London: Methuen, 1985.

Molinaro, Nina. "Resistance, Gender, and the Mediation of History in Pizarnik's *La condesa sangrienta* and Ortiz's *Urraca.*" *Letras Femeninas* 19.1–2 (1993): 45–54.

———. "The Simulacra of Power: *El amor es un juego solitario.*" *Foucault, Feminism and Power: Reading Esther Tusquets.* Lewisburg, Pa.: Bucknell University Press, 1991. 42–55.

Moliner, María. *Diccionario de uso del español.* Madrid: Gredos, 1994.

Montero, Rosa. *La hija del Caníbal.* Madrid: Espasa, 1997.

———. "The Silent Revolution: The Social and Cultural Advances of Women in Democratic Spain." In *Spanish Cultural Studies.* Ed. Helen Graham and Jo Labanyi. Oxford: Oxford University Press, 1995. 381–86.

Mora, Gabriela. "Escritura erótica: Cristina Peri Rossi y Tununa Mercado." In *Carnal Knowledge: Essays on the Flesh, Sex, and Sexuality in Hispanic Letters and Film.* Ed. Pamela Bacarisse. Pittsburgh: Tres Ríos, 1991. 129–40.

Morales Villena, Gregorio. "Entrevista con Lourdes Ortiz." *Insula* 41.479 (1986): 1, 10.

Moret, Xavier. "La joven Lucía Etxebarría recibe el Nadal con una novela que trata de la iniciación sexual." *El País,* 7 Jan. 1998, 28.

———. "'Me presenté al Nadal para suavizar la reacción de mis padres a mi novela.'" *El País,* 1 Aug. 1998, 28.

Morris, Barbara, and Lou Charnon-Deutsch. "Regarding the Pornographic Subject in *Las edades de Lulú.*" *Letras Peninsulares* 6.2–3 (1993): 301–19.

Moxey, Keith. *The Practice of Theory: Poststructuralism, Cultural Politics, and Art History.* Ithaca: Cornell University Press, 1994.

Mulvey, Laura. *Fetishism and Curiosity.* Bloomington: Indiana University Press, 1996.

Navajas, Gonzalo. "Duplicidad narrativa en *Las edades de Lulú* de Almudena Grandes." In *Studies in Honor of Gilberto Paolini.* Ed. Mercedes Vidal Tibbitts. Newark, Del.: Juan de la Cuesta, 1996. 385–92.

Works Cited

Nichols, Geraldine Cleary. "Caída/Re(s)puesta: La narrative femenina de la posguerra." In *Literatura y vida cotidiana: Actas de las cuartas jornadas de investigación interdisciplinaria.* Ed. María Ángeles and José Antonio Rey. Zaragoza: Universidad Autónoma de Madrid, 1987. 325–35.

———. "Minding Her P's and Q's: The Fiction of Esther Tusquets." *Indiana Journal of Hispanic Literatures* 2.1 (1993): 159–79.

———. "Mitja poma, mitja taronja: Genesis y destino literarios de la catalana contemporánea." *Anthropos* (Apr.–May 1986) 118–25.

Noñi, Ana. "Entrevista a Cristina Peri Rossi." *Quimera* 185 (1999): 9–13.

Obligado, Clara. *La hija de Marx.* Barcelona: Lumen, 1996.

———. *Si un hombre te hace llorar.* Barcelona: Planeta, 1998.

Ordóñez, Elizabeth. "Inscribing Difference: 'L'Ecriture féminine' and New Narrative by Women." *Anales de la Literatura Española Contemporánea* 12.1–2 (1987): 45–58.

———. "Reading Contemporary Spanish Narrative by Women." *Anales de la Literatura Española Contemporánea* 7.2 (1982): 237–51.

———. *Voices of Their Own: Contemporary Spanish Narrative by Women.* Lewisburg, Pa.: Bucknell University Press, 1991.

Ortega Bargueño, Pilar. "Almudena Grandes: 'La etiqueta de escritora erótica fue fácil de soportar.'" *El Mundo,* 18 June 2001, <http://www.elmundo.es>.

Ortiz, Lourdes. *Urraca.* Madrid: Debate, 1991.

Pérez, Janet. *Contemporary Women Writers of Spain.* Boston: Twayne, 1988.

Pérez-Sánchez, Gema. "Entrevista: Cristina Peri Rossi." *Hispamérica: Revista de Literatura* 24.72 (1995): 59–72.

Peri Rossi, Cristina. *Desastres íntimos.* Barcelona: Lumen, 1997.

———. *El amor es una droga dura.* Barcelona: Seix Barral, 2000.

———. *Fantasías eróticas.* Madrid: Temas de Hoy, 1992.

———. *Inmovilidad de los barcos.* Vitoria: Bassarai, 1997.

———. *Solitario de amor.* Barcelona: Grijalbo, 1988.

Phelan, Peggy. *Unmarked: The Politics of Performance.* London: Routledge, 1993.

Porter, Phoebe. "Conversación con Lourdes Ortiz." *Letras Femeninas* 16.1–2 (1990): 139–44.

Readings, Bill. *Introducing Lyotard: Art and Politics.* London: Routledge, 1991.

Riera, Miguel. "Cristina Peri Rossi: Médium de sí." *Quimera* 151 (October 1996): 15–24.

Rimmon-Kenan, Shlomith. *Narrative Fiction: Contemporary Poetics.* London: Routledge, 1983.

Rivas, B. "El éxito de Lulú." *El Mundo,* 15 June 1990, 1–2.

Rivera Villegas, Carmen M. "Cuerpo, palabra y autodescubrimiento en *Urraca,* de Lourdes Ortiz." *Bulletin of Hispanic Studies* 74.3 (1997): 307–14.

Rodríguez, Juan María. "Peri Rossi y Matute debaten la existencia de una literatura femenina." *El País,* 25 Nov. 1994, 37.

———. "Soledad Puértolas critica la falta de grandes personajes femeninos en los libros de hoy." *El País,* 26 Nov. 1994, 29.

Rowinsky, Mercedes. *Imagen y discurso: Estudio de las imágenes en la obra de Cristina Peri Rossi.* Montevideo: Trilce, 1997.

Sánchez García, Rufino, et al., eds. *Informe SGAE: Sobre hábitos de consumo cultural.* Madrid: Sociedad General de Autores de España, 2000.

Santos, Care. *El tango del perdedor.* Barcelona: Alba, 1997

———. *Trigal con cuervos.* Sevilla: Algaida, 1999.

Sanz Villanueva, Santos. "Lucía Etxebarría: *Beatriz y los cuerpos celestes.*" *La Esfera,* 14 Feb. 1998, 15.

Sieburth, Stephanie. *Inventing High and Low: Literature, Mass Culture, and Uneven Modernity in Spain.* Durham: Duke University Press, 1994.

Silverman, Kaja. *The Subject of Semiotics.* New York: Oxford University Press, 1983.

———. *The Threshold of the Visible World.* New York: Routledge, 1996.

Solomon-Godeau, Abigail. "The Other Side of Venus: The Visual Economy of Feminine Display." In *The Sex of Things: Gender and Consumption in Historical Perspective.* Ed. Victoria de Grazia and Ellen Furlough. Berkeley: University of California Press, 1996. 113–50

Spires, Robert. *Post-Totalitarian Spanish Fiction.* Columbia: University of Missouri Press, 1996.

Steele, Valerie. *Fetish: Fashion, Sex, and Power.* New York: Oxford University Press, 1996.

Steiner, Wendy. *The Scandal of Pleasure: Art in the Age of Fundamentalism.* Chicago: University of Chicago Press, 1995.

Stratton, Jon. *The Desirable Body: Cultural Fetishism and the Erotics of Consumption.* Manchester: Manchester University Press, 1996.

Talbot, Lynn. "Lourdes Ortiz's *Urraca:* A Re-vision/Revision of History." *Romance Quarterly* 38.4 (1991): 437–48.

Terrell, Peter. *Collins German/English, English/German Dictionary: Unabridged.* New York: HarperCollins, 1999.

Threlfall, Monica, ed. *Mapping the Women's Movement: Feminist Politics and Social Transformation in the North.* New York: Verso, 1996.

Thwaites, Lilit. "Historical Truth and 'Real' Truth: A Case of History and 'Her' Story in *Urraca* and *Anillos para una dama.*" In *War and Revolution in Hispanic Literature.* Ed. Roy Boland and Alun Kenwood. Madrid: Voz Hispánica, 1990. 211–19.

Tusquets, Esther. *El amor es un juego solitario.* Barcelona: Lumen, 1979.

Vásquez, Mary S., ed. *The Sea of Becoming: Approaches to the Fiction of Esther Tusquets.* New York: Greenwood Press, 1991.

Vázquez, Juana. "De ejecutivas, marujas y 'modelos.'" *El Mundo,* 4 Dec. 1997, <http://www.elmundolibro.es>.

Verani, Hugo. "La rebelión del cuerpo y el lenguaje." In *Cristina Peri Rossi, papeles críticos.* Ed. Rómulo Cosse et al. Montevideo: Linardi y Risso, 1995. 9–21.

Vidal, Nuria. "Lucía Etxebarría: Con ella llegó el escándalo." *Qué Leer,* Mar. 1998, 42–46.

Villamor, Manuel. "Almudena Grandes, *Las edades de Lulú.*" *El Nuevo Lunes,* 31 Dec. 1990, 46.

Villanueva, Darío, et al. "La restauración de la narratividad." In *Historia y crítica de la literatura española: Los nuevos nombres, 1975–1990.* Ed. Francisco Rico. Barcelona: Crítica, 1992. 285–92.

Von Fries, Fritz Rudolf. "Liliths Töchter: Lucía Etxebarrías Provokationsroman 'Von Liebe, Neugier, Prozac, und Zweifel.'" *Frankfurter Rundschau,* 7 Nov. 1998, 4.

Wright, Elizabeth, ed. *Feminism and Psychoanalysis: A Critical Dictionary.* Cambridge: Blackwell, 1992.

Zunzunegui, Santos. *Desear el deseo: Publicidad, consumo y comportamiento.* Bilbao: Universidad del País Vasco, 1990.

Index

Index

Index

Index

Index

CHRISTINE HENSELER is an assistant professor of Spanish in the Department of Modern Languages and Literatures at Union College. She specializes in contemporary Peninsular narrative, women's studies, and cultural studies with a particular interest in visual culture and media studies.

Hispanisms

The University of Illinois Press
is a founding member of the
Association of American University Presses.

Composed in 10.5/13 Minion
with Caflish display and Arabesque Ornaments
by Type One, LLC
for the University of Illinois Press
Designed by Dennis Roberts
Manufactured by Thomson-Shore, Inc.
University of Illinois Press

1325 South Oak Street
Champaign, IL 61820-6903
www.press.uillinois.edu